Greenhouse Gardening

An Extensive Guide Including Process to Build your Greenhouse System and Grow Healthy Vegetables, Fruits, Plants, and Herbs.

By

Thomas Watergreen

© Copyright 2020 Thomas Watergreen- All rights reserved.

The content contained within this book may not be reproduced, duplicated, or transmitted without direct written permission from the author or the publisher.

Under no circumstances will any blame or legal responsibility be held against the publisher, or author, for any damages, reparation, or monetary loss due to the information contained within this book. Either directly or indirectly.

Legal Notice:

This book is copyright protected. This book is only for personal use. You cannot amend, distribute, sell, use, quote, or paraphrase any part, or the content within this book, without the consent of the author or publisher.

Disclaimer Notice:

Please note that the information contained within this document is for educational and entertainment purposes only. All effort has been executed to present accurate, up to date, and reliable, complete information. No warranties of any kind are declared or implied. Readers acknowledge that the author is not engaging in the rendering of legal, financial, medical, or professional advice. The content within this book has been derived from various sources. Please consult a licensed professional before attempting any techniques outlined in this book.

By reading this document, the reader agrees that under no circumstances is the author responsible for any losses, direct or indirect, which are incurred as a result of the use of the information contained within this document, including, but not limited to, — errors, omissions, or inaccuracies.

Table of contents

INTRODUCTION 7

What Is a Greenhouse 7

Basics of Greenhouse Gardening.. 7

How Greenhouses Work.. 8

Different Forms of Greenhouses.. 9

CHAPTER 1: HOW A GREENHOUSE CAN BENEFIT YOU 13

CHAPTER 2: PLANNING FOR A GREENHOUSE 17

2.1 How to draw up a Plan..17

2.2 Making a Gardening Schedule...17

2.3 Listing out Materials..18

2.4 Site Preparation 20

CHAPTER 3: PORTABLE GREENHOUSES 21

CHAPTER 4: HEATING YOUR GREENHOUSE................. 28

4.1 Where to Put Your Heater 31

4.2 Mains Gas Heating 34

4.3 Greenhouse Heating Tips...34

CHAPTER 5: GREENHOUSE PROBLEMS........................... 38

5.1 Potential Greenhouse Problems..38

5.2 The Most Common Greenhouse Mistake 39

CHAPTER 6: BUYING A USED GREENHOUSE 41

CHAPTER 7: GREENHOUSE IRRIGATION SYSTEMS 46

7.1 Different Irrigation Systems in Greenhouses 46

7.2 Advantages of the Greenhouse Irrigation System 49

7.3 Grow Stronger Plants with a Good Greenhouse Watering System 51

CHAPTER 8: PESTS AND DISEASES 53

8.1 Pests and Disease Control 53

8.2 Pest Management 53

8.3 Maintaining Greenhouse Hygiene 54

8.4 Use Disease-Free Plants 55

8.5 Control the Growing Environment 55

8.6 Control Entry to the Greenhouse 56

8.7 Tips for Pest and Disease Control 56

8.8 Integrated Pest Management Techniques 57

8.9 Identify the Type of Pests Affecting the Crops 58

8.10 Control Measures 60

8.11 Disease Preventive Measures 61

8.12 Common Greenhouse Diseases 62

CHAPTER 9: BUILD A SOLID FOUNDATION 65

9.1 Choosing the Correct Foundation 65

9.2 Preparing the Site for a Greenhouse 66

9.3 Top-Notch Materials for the Best Foundation 67

9.4 Taking Steps to a Solid Foundation 67

CHAPTER 10: STARTING SEEDS 69

CHAPTER 11: USEFUL GREENHOUSE EQUIPMENT 76

11.1 Digging Utensils 76

11.2 Cultivating tools 77

11.3 Cutting Tools 78

CHAPTER 12: HOW TO GROW WITHOUT SOIL 81

12.1 How Does Hydroponics Work? 81

CHAPTER 13: GREENHOUSE ENVIRONMENTAL CONTROL SYSTEMS 85

13.1 Accessories Controlled 85

13.2 Advantages of Automated System 86

13.3 Advanced Accessories 86

13.4 Advanced Ventilation 89

13.5 Advance Watering Systems 90

13.6 Greenhouse Shelving 92

CHAPTER 14: 15 TIPS TO MAKE YOUR GREENHOUSE MORE EFFICIENT 94

CHAPTER 15: MAINTAINING YOUR GREENHOUSE 99

15.1 How to maintain the right Temperature in the Greenhouse 100

15.2 How to maintain the right relative Humidity in a Greenhouse 100

15.3 Maintaining your Greenhouse in Cold weather 101

CONCLUSION 103

Introduction

What Is a Greenhouse

A greenhouse is an age-old structure that is designed to retain heat, absorb light, and protect plants within. It can be the source for your summer starts, or it can be an option for a winter garden for year-round produce.

These simple structures have thin, transparent walls made of glass, plastic panels, or plastic sheeting supported by metal, wood, or plastic structure. The skeleton is often lightweight and durable, yet strong enough to support the intended exterior. Each is designed to allow the maximum amount of light and retain as much heat and humidity as possible.

Greenhouses have changed over time to meet specific needs – large or small. A greenhouse can be as small as a plastic bottle over a seedling or as large as a multi-acre building on a massive cash crop. They can be domes or have steep pitches, lean-tos, or standalone structures. But, while the design and materials may vary, the intent is always the same: grow plants in the best environment possible.

Because of the heat dynamics of a greenhouse, it's possible to extend the growing season for plants to meet the need of a market. It may mean the success of your garden annuals, the potential for year-round food production, or a safe place to harbor plants until they are strong enough to survive outdoors.

Basics of Greenhouse Gardening

Greenhouse gardening is based on a steady temperature to stop plants from exposure to many of the problems that generally don't lead to success.

An icy environment, wind, rain, heat, and weeds can be fended off with an adequate greenhouse structure.

Once built, it is easy to monitor growth and provide any other needs using utilities and other environmental controls. Water can be either manually or automatically provided through hand watering, drip lines, spray systems, or sprinklers. Lights can provide longer growing times when the sun isn't out. Ventilation is used to increase or decrease the humidity and regulate heat within the greenhouse.

Checking the environment allows you to plant off-seasons and reproduce any type of weather for your plants. The lack of extremes helps plants during the first few days through full-cycle production. Extensive greenhouses are extremely ergonomic because the elevated plant beds are located above ground level so they can be easier to manage, rotate, and care for; this differs from traditional gardening in that the plants aren't sown directly in the soil. Alternatively, they are planted in a particular soil till they grow enough to be transported outdoors, or into larger pots to continue growth indoors.

Greenhouse growing has created a new path for improved forms of cultivation like vertical gardens, hydroponics, aquaponics, and large-scale production of organic food sources. The greenhouse is often easier to maintain than a typical garden because of fewer variables, ease of upkeep, and a more stable environment.

How Greenhouses Work

Greenhouses work on a straightforward principle – trap heat and absorb sunlight. The shape and the materials in a greenhouse do create this effect. Greenhouses allow for light, hold on to warmth, and help the gardener protecting the plants.

Energy from the sun in the form of gleaming heat and lights are irradiated inside of the greenhouse. The greenhouse walls absorb the light and radiate heat. Then, the greenhouse blocks the warmth from exiting. On the contrary, heat is absorbed and retained within. As heat is retained, it rises and prevents air movement, and the entire structure remains at a constant temperature until heat is expelled by way of ventilators and holes. The air temperature outside the greenhouse doesn't affect the heat inside, even if the external temperature is cold.

Because plants grow in sustained and steady environments, greenhouses are still a simple yet effective way to provide an ideal space for growth. When there is no sunlight, alternative artificial lighting can provide an optimum substitute to help plants in their growth. When rain is not available, water may be provided in the form of irrigation or by hand.

Different Forms of Greenhouses

Even Span

Even Span is the most typical design people consider when it comes to greenhouses. The name describes the construction in that the roofline has an even span from the center peak to the eaves, and this pitch runs the full length of the structure. Regardless of how deep the structure is, the Even Span design allows for a continuous, simple rectangular layout inside.

The design allows for maximum direct sunlight from above. It is very efficient and provides a significant amount of space for plants inside. It's also easy to build, structurally sound, and provides enough slope to allow rainwater water runoff. The American style has a single, taller peak where a similar Dutch style has two peaks along the same span. When combined eave to eave, these structures resemble a row home or townhouse and are known as a Ridge and Furrow.

Because every square foot within the base of the greenhouse can be used for plant growth, these structures are an excellent option for massive operations. It is easy to expand in any direction, as long as the terrain is flat and level on grade.

Lean-To

For existing structures like houses or commercial buildings, a lean-to structure is another option. These are generally connected to the side of an exterior wall. The roof is then sloped downward away from the structure it is connected to, and a shorter wall supports the eave. The two gable end halves are enclosed with flat wall support and sealed with the same material as the rest of the structure.

These structures are best used on southern-facing walls to allow the most significant amount of sunlight in – especially during winter months. Because these aren't part of the original structure, and they rely on the existing structure to provide some of the support, the Lean-To greenhouse may require some level of permitting and engineering.

One of the main benefits of the Lean-To structure is the ease of access. Because these are often built as additions to existing homes, it is possible to walk directly out of a residence and step into the greenhouse; this eliminates the need to cross vast distances to the garden as the garden may be located right outside the main structure.

- **Free Standing**

Free Standing Greenhouses are generally those that are commercially available and engineered to withstand the forces of nature without additional structural support. Some free-standing greenhouses look similar to the even span design, while others resemble a geodesic dome or Quonset hut. Regardless of the shape, these are meant to host a limited number of plants and are generally large enough for one person to work comfortably inside.

The main benefit of a Free-Standing Greenhouse is the ability to set it up on your own without special permitting, skills, or tools. Additional perks include a limited footprint that provides the benefits of a greenhouse in areas with limited space, limited portability if it needs to be relocated, and lower cost. These structures are generally a solid choice for the average homeowner or tenant.

Because these are often assembled on-site, they may or may not have components designed for power or water; this means you may need to supply utilities with extension cords, hoses, or solar systems.

- "A"- Frame

In areas where snow load is a significant concern, the A-Frame greenhouse provides a stable environment in all types of weather. This structure is designed with a steep pitch that sheds snow on the outer edges and prevents build-up on the roof. The roof extends from the peak to the ground and can be mounded up on the edges to add support in areas with high winds.

The A-Frame uses a steeper structure to allow more sun when it is lower on the horizon during winter months; this allows more access to heat and fewer opportunities for extreme weather failure. Some useable space is lost due to the low edges, and some of the higher areas generate some wasted space. However, these are an ideal option in northern zones.

Because of the design, they can be constructed with translucent plastic sheeting and still produce the same effect as glass or plastic panels. As snow builds at the base of the triangle formed by the roof, it helps to insulate and protect the outer edges from extreme cold and high winds.

- **Domes and Huts**

An emerging style of greenhouse is proving a natural fit for cost and space limitations. Geodesic domes are a structurally sound dome made of interlocking isosceles triangle sections. These are identical to a climbing dome you might see on a playground, except they are covered in clear plastic or glass panels. They can be scaled up to just about any size without impacting the structure and provide a significant amount of space that is not encumbered by additional structural supports or beams.

Huts also provide a form of greenhouse that can be scaled up or down depending on the need and space available. Sometimes referred to as Quonset huts, these half-cylinders create a long, tall structure that can withstand heavy snow loads and wind. They can be as small as a few feet in size, or they can provide enough space to house a multi-story structure. The arched structural supports may be engineered trusses or basic PVC pipe, and wall coverings are often a heavy-duty clear membrane or clear plastic sheeting.

Chapter 1: How a Greenhouse Can Benefit You

A greenhouse can be a significant investment though you can find used greenhouses cheap or even free if you are willing to dismantle them and replace a few panes.

With a greenhouse, you are creating a micro-environment in which you have control over the climate.

Greenhouses typically have a wooden or aluminum frame and usually glass or toughened plastic panes. Materials are essential but decisions about them depend on the location and the intended use of your greenhouse.

For now, though, let's talk about how a greenhouse benefits you, which always helps in justifying the expense and time to assemble it!

Longer Growing Seasons

For people who live north of the equator, growing seasons never seem long enough. Even a distance of 40 miles further north can significantly alter the length of the growing season enough that you can't grow your favorite plants (trust me in that, it's devastating to realize that some plants are now a struggle to grow).

Plants that were grown in a greenhouse enjoy a much warmer environment, which means you can lengthen your growing time by a month or more on either end of the season. With a heater, you can lengthen it even further!

Greenhouses trap the sun's radiation, which means it gets hot in a greenhouse, allowing you to grow plants that you would otherwise be unable to grow outside. For me, it means I can not only grow tomatoes but have a long enough growing season for them to ripen and taste delicious!

Protection from the Elements

The climate is very changeable, and you can experience a heatwave and hail within the same week! This variation in weather can cause many problems with your plants and stunt their growth. Squashes, in particular, are susceptible to low growth and will not produce female flowers if the weather is too cold.

When you grow in a greenhouse, you protect your plants from this variation in weather as well as damage from late frosts and high winds. It also protects your plants from torrential rain and getting too waterlogged.

It gives your plants a fighting chance, even if you only start them off in the greenhouse before moving them to a permanent site in the soil elsewhere on your vegetable plot.

With a greenhouse, you can be smug that your plants are safe while other gardeners are worried about the damage from extreme weather.

Saving on Grocery Expenses

Yes, you can save money on your grocery bill by growing fruits and vegetables that are expensive in the stores. Being able to grow earlier and later in the year means you can get more produce out of the growing season.

In most cases, a greenhouse owner makes back the cost of the greenhouse in grocery savings within two or even three years of purchase!

Consistent Growing Environment

Many plants hate an inconsistent growing environment. When it is hot one day and cold the next, then dry for a week before flooding, your plants quite naturally get upset and don't grow well.

The advantage of a greenhouse is that your plants are insulated from climatic variations, and so they grow much better, maturing faster and often producing a far better crop. So we can easily say that your planning is no longer going to be ruined by the weather.

Plant Protection

Most vegetable plants are relatively weak when compared to weeds. Just look at how quickly weeds grow compared to your precious vegetables. Your plants grow much more robust and faster because they do not have to compete with weeds for resources.

A greenhouse protects your plants not only from the climate but also from seasonal pests such as locusts or Japanese beetles and, to a degree, from wind-borne diseases.

Optimal Growing Environment

As a gardener, you know that many vegetable plants prefer a warm, humid environment to grow. Tomatoes, in particular, like heat to ripen, and without the right temperature, don't turn red.

In a greenhouse, you can give your plants the optimal growing environment, which helps them to produce an excellent crop for you.

Season Free Gardening

Don't you hate it when you suddenly think about planting something and realize that you can't because it is the wrong season? Or maybe you see the season drawing to a close, and your vegetables aren't quite ripe yet?

With a greenhouse, you have control over the climate, and so with the right heater, fan, and ventilation, you can start your seasonal plants early or extend your growing season so your vegetables can ripen fully.

All-Weather Gardening

Before I got a greenhouse, I would either get wet if it was raining or not tend to my vegetable plot. With a greenhouse, I can potter around and do something even when it is raining, which is rather pleasant.

It's a significant benefit to being able to do this as being able to continue to do some work even in inclement weather is a real boon.

Multi-purpose Gardening

The lovely thing about a greenhouse is you are not just limited to growing tomatoes; you can grow anything you want!

I've seen people growing herbs, cactus plants, and even bonsai trees in their greenhouse! I've just moved my cacti to my greenhouse as they are too big for the house!

The mix of plants you grow doesn't matter because they are grown in pots rather than directly in the soil; this means you can grow just about anything and mix both indoor and outdoor plants without any problems!

As you can see, there are a whole host of benefits of owning a greenhouse. With all the advantages and benefits, it is a must-have for any gardener and will help you to grow more plants, get better crops, and get more from your vegetable plot!

Chapter 2: Planning For a Greenhouse

2.1 How to draw up a Plan

To get started with your greenhouse, first come up with an appropriate plan. To do this, you'll need to consider your purpose, your space, and your environment. These three factors play a vital role in the type and size of greenhouse you'll want to build.

Your purpose is unique to you and what you intend to grow. Small flowers, herbs, and microgreens require a different level of care compared to a large-scale grow operation or winter garden meant for a family food source. Determine what your need is, then survey the space you'll need to achieve your harvest goals within the greenhouse.

Once you know what your purpose is, you can establish a footprint for your greenhouse. Survey the space you have available and the orientation that works best. Your purpose will drive the space required for your greenhouse. Pick a flat, level surface, or find an area that can be cleared for a structure.

Once you've decided on your purpose and the amount of space you'll need, you can draw up plans based on the type of structure that suits your location. You'll want to make sure the footprint and design are suitable for weather patterns in your area. Specifics about site preparation and construction are covered.

2.2 Making a Gardening Schedule

Because greenhouses are useful in extreme heat or cold, they provide a rare opportunity for year-round plant growth.

You can take advantage of this by keeping a garden schedule and rotating plants as they grow to keep a constant source of new starts and plants that can be harvested.

To start a garden schedule, determine the full bloom or harvest date and work backward. For example, if you want to grow tomatoes ready for mid-winter, start planting in the greenhouse 4-6 months prior. If you intend to transplant or sell plants that are still growing during early summer months, start in late winter or early spring. Your plants dictate when you need to get seeds in the soil based on when you want a substantial harvest. If you're looking for a regular harvest on a daily, weekly, or monthly basis, simply start a new batch of seeds spaced out as desired from the previous one.

The daily schedule within the greenhouse depends on the available daylight and access to utilities. You can provide lights, water, or ventilation on elaborate timers, or control these variables by hand. Ideally, it is best to take advantage of natural sunlight as much as possible, so consider the lighting on a consistent start and stop time that can supplement the natural solar cycle throughout a day. Plants thrive on varying light cycles, so pay close attention to the needs of your plants and move them within your greenhouse to each progressive light station as needed to generate the best results.

2.3 Listing out Materials

If you're building a greenhouse from scratch, you can determine how much materials you'll need by modeling a similar structure and doing some basic math. The main components within a greenhouse are:

- Structure
- Skin/walls
- Water

- Power
- Flooring

Depending on the type of structure you choose as a framework, you'll need to determine how many supports, uprights, trusses, cross-members, and joints are required. The span from one structural member to another depends on the type of material you use on the exterior walls and roof. The structure is going to be the sum of all linear dimensions of supports, trusses, and beams. Keep in mind that you'll also need to consider the materials required to fasten structural components together.

The skin on roofing and walls is determined by taking the length multiplied by the width or height. Gable ends and roof pitch calculations require basic geometry to determine how much will be needed. Multiply the roof pitch on each side by the length of the structure to determine the roof footage. Domes require more complex calculations to determine the surface area of the sphere.

Once you have your structure and wall materials quantified, determine your water delivery plans. If you are using sprinklers, drip lines, misters, or other methods of providing water, you'll need to map out piping, elbows, joints, valves, hoses, and heads for each. Even if you only intend to hand-water your plants, make sure you have a good source for water – during all forms of weather – and a means for watering your plants.

Power delivery is another challenge to keep in mind. If you intend to provide lighting or ventilation, make sure you have enough bulbs, fixtures, outlets, fans, vents, and monitors or controls. It may require electrical work performed by tradesmen to provide power to the structure, or it may be a matter of running an extension cord from another structure to the greenhouse.

List out any power delivery materials along with the materials that may consume power.

If you intend to pour a concrete pad or create some other form of the substrate beneath your greenhouse, determine the footprint of your structure, then multiply it by the thickness of the floor you intend to create. This allows you to obtain materials based on volume. Add any materials used for the framework around the perimeter to your list.

2.4 Site Preparation

With your purpose in mind and your materials in hand, it's time to get your site ready to build. You should have determined a significant location with adequate sunlight and a relatively flat area.

Some obstacles may dictate where you can locate your greenhouse. Structures, steep hillsides, and shade trees can limit where you set your site up. However, if you can modify your terrain with power tools or heavy equipment, these obstacles won't stand in your way.

Provide an ideal site location by leveling out the substrate; this requires removal of plants, shrubs, or trees, and could involve moving significant amounts of dirt. You can save yourself some work by setting up your greenhouse in an area that is flat, open to the sun, and away from tall shade-producing trees or structures that could interfere with natural light.

With a flat, level surface, you can then install concrete footings or a full pad designed to bear the weight of your structure. Concrete pads are easier to maintain and keep clean. A level, a solid foundation provides the best results and allow your structure to withstand the harsh natural forces that are likely to act upon it.

Chapter 3: Portable Greenhouses

Greenhouses come in all shapes and sizes. Some pay others to build one for them. Others buy kits and assemble the greenhouse themselves. These options can be quite expensive. The truth is that most people can buy inexpensive supplies and build their greenhouse from scratch. You can also do so in such a way that at the end of the growing season, it can quickly be taken down if you so desire.

The best reason to have a greenhouse is to extend the growing season. Maybe you live in a part of the country that is prone to late spring freezes. Maybe you have early winters where you live. Maybe you would like to grow some winter vegetables, but may not be able to without the protection that a greenhouse offers. A greenhouse can both protect from freezing temperatures and provide sufficient heat for plant growth that would not exist if your vegetables were simply out in the open and subject to the elements/air temperature. A greenhouse can also offer your crops protection from hail and other inclement weather. You may even be able to grow crops that typically could not survive in your area.

There are a couple of main reasons why people who like to garden may not take advantage of the benefits that a greenhouse offers. The costs and others turn some off because, for weather or other reasons, they do not want a greenhouse up all year round. In regards to cost, the models I suggest are of minimal cost. Some who live in areas that typically receive snow, hail, and other bad weather may not want a greenhouse up year-round. If that is a concern for you, the models I propose can relatively easily be deconstructed.

I am not recommending specific sizes for the frame of your greenhouse. That is up to you. Some people who usually have a large area of vegetables in their back yard may want a large greenhouse; others who only want to grow one or two crops may choose a smaller greenhouse, possibly on their side yard, between their house and fence or another small area.

Some people may design/construct their greenhouse in such a way that it has tables or other raised platforms to grow their plants on. Such construction may be appropriate when constructing an expensive greenhouse that one never intends to remove, and if the person has back problems and cannot get on the ground to the garden. Such design is not appropriate for an inexpensive greenhouse that you intend to deconstruct at the end of each growing season. The greenhouses that follow are intended to cover plants that are growing directly in the ground.

The first thing you need to decide is which material to use for the frame of your inexpensive greenhouse. The two best choices are a white PVC pipe like you would use for an outdoor lawn watering system. The other option is untreated wooden 2 X 4's. Don't use treated lumber because the wood should not be exposed to water and because even if water leaks onto your wooden frame, you do not want chemicals from treated lumber leaching into the ground and onto your crops. If you have back problems, arthritis, or other physical ailments that make lifting and bending a problem, a plastic PVC pipe is the better choice for you. If you live in an area that typically gets strong winds in the spring, summer, or fall, wood may be a better choice for your frame. You could also combine wooden 2 X 4's and PVC for your frame where you use wood for the bottom and PVC for the sides/roof.

Let us begin by discussing a PVC frame. You can go to your local home improvement store and buy this type in ten-foot lengths. The most convenient shape to fashion this into a greenhouse is an oval or egg-shaped greenhouse. If you want a somewhat broad and tall greenhouse, you could use two ten-piece PVC pipes, one on each side, and connecting them at the roof of the greenhouse. How many of these you need it to be determined by how long you want your greenhouse to go. I also recommend you have one piece of PVC pipe running lengthwise along the roof to fasten the side pieces. This increases the structural integrity of the greenhouse. You can join the connections with PVC connectors, zip ties, or even duct tape in a pinch. Then on one side of the greenhouse, fashion a door frame out of PVC pipe, as well as a door with lengths of PVC running width wise and height wise. The door can be fastened to the frame using zip ties.

Wooden 2 X 4's are the other practical and inexpensive option for this type of greenhouse frame. Some people use a combination of wood and PVC pipe. If this is what you want to do, I recommend you use wood for the base around the edges of your greenhouse, as well as the front where you insert a door, and the back. With this combination of materials, you can still make the oval-shaped sides and roof.

The other option is to make a greenhouse frame entirely out of wood. Most people do not shape greenhouse like an oval, instead build the sides and roof like an A frame shape with the sides directly straight up perpendicular to the ground and the two sides of the roof coming together like the shape of the letter A, much like the shape of a roof on most residential house. I should note here that sometimes people who construct their greenhouse entirely out of PVC pipe also construct it in the A-frame fashion instead of an oval shape, but the oval shape is more prevalent when using an entire PVC pipe for the frame.

One potential disadvantage of using wood to construct your greenhouse frame is the potential for sharp edges to damage the greenhouse plastic used for the windows. Accordingly, if you use wood, try to make sure the pieces fit together well, and you may need to take a power sander to sand off any sharp edges.

If using wood, construct a door out of wood, and construct a wooden frame around the door. Attach the door to the frame with metal hinges and screws. You could install an inexpensive doorknob like you would use on an interior door of a house to keep your wooden door closed.

It would help if you decided how far apart to space your side supports, which create the walls of your greenhouse. I recommend every two and a half to three feet. If using wood, you might be tempted to space them further apart because you would think wood is more robust than PVC, and therefore you do not need as many supports. I would resist this temptation because the purpose of the PVC or wood is not only to hold the frame together but to give adequate support to the plastic sheeting used as windows.

When constructing your greenhouse frame out of wood, you could use screws or nails to fasten the pieces of wood together. When deconstructing the greenhouse, if you used screws to fasten the wood together, you should be able to remove the screws with a screw gun relatively quickly. If you intend to use nails, I recommend you use nails designed for laying form boards for concrete. These nails have two heads, one that is pounded down to the base of the wood, and the other that is left exposed to make removing the nail much more manageable once the concrete is set and the form boards are then removed.

Once your frame is complete, you are ready to wrap the frame in plastic greenhouse sheeting. Take care when attaching the sheeting so that you do not cut or tear it. This process is easier/faster if you have one person on each side of the greenhouse. If you have a third person standing around doing nothing, you could even have them stand in the middle of the greenhouse. The greenhouse might be tall enough that that person in the middle might not be able to reach the sheeting with their hands. They could use a soft mop to reach up and help push the sheeting down the length of the greenhouse as the two people on both sides pull the sheeting. Start at one end of the greenhouse, pull the plastic sheeting up and over and then pull it down the greenhouse.

It is then time to fasten your plastic sheeting to the bottom of the frame. It should be fastened somewhat tight, but not so tight that it cannot move a little bit, which it will need to do when the temperature changes. Extend it over your greenhouse and slightly past the bottom of the greenhouse. You could use screws to fasten the sheeting to the bottom of the greenhouse frame. You could also use staples. There are also specific types of tape just for this purpose, such as polypropylene batten tape. Wiring is an additional option. If using PVC for your frame, an additional way to fasten the plastic is to use one size PVC for the frame, and pieces of a larger sized PVC, cut in half, and then snap those bigger pieces over the plastic and onto the frame. For example, let us say you used a half-inch PVC for the frame. Once you wrap the frame in plastic sheeting, you could then cut 3/4 inch PVC in half and take one half and snap it over the plastic and onto the 1/2 PVC frame.

Construct your greenhouse early in the spring, so you are ready to plant early on. Remember that with a greenhouse, you can plant your crops earlier than usual because of the warmth it will create. If living in a region with below-freezing temperatures, obviously, you will not be able to plant so long as the ground is still frozen. Setting up your greenhouse may help the ground below your greenhouse thaw quicker than it otherwise would. Also, if you do intend to set up a table or other platform and put plants on top of it, waiting for the ground to thaw is not such a concern.

At the end of the growing season, you are now in a position to easily deconstruct your greenhouse. On the other hand, some people build this type of greenhouse but then decide for a variety of reasons to leave the greenhouse up. If you do this, I still recommend you remove the plastic greenhouse sheeting.

How long will your plastic sheeting last? If it is quality sheeting, and it has not been damaged during the growing season, there is no reason you could not get three years or more of use out of it. In order for this to happen, you should carefully remove it at the end of each growing season. Carefully remove the screws, staples, wires, or whatever you used to fasten the sheeting and then gingerly roll it up. Before reinstalling the sheeting before the next growing season, wash the sheeting with soap and warm water to remove dirt, dead bugs, and the like, so that it will be clear enough to let sufficient light through.

Your total costs in constructing your greenhouse will be determined based on how big/long you decide to make your greenhouse. I would expect for a typical one you might construct in your urban/suburban back yard, you can do so for less than $200. This money will be quickly offset when you start picking produce in your backyard instead of buying it at the supermarket.

Some people do something else with a small portable greenhouse. They use it only as a starter of sorts. Let us say, for example, they want to grow tomatoes. Maybe they normally plant them at the beginning of June, but they would like to plant them early. They plant them on May 1st and immediately cover them with a small PVC greenhouse like the one mentioned here. Then around June 1st or June 15th, when the weather is much warmer, and the sun is blazing hot, they remove the greenhouse. They only needed the greenhouse to extend the growing season at the beginning of the season.

Greenhouses do not have to be expensive or permanent. For a small investment, most people can fairly easily construct a portable greenhouse that will extend their growing season, and that can easily be removed at the end of the growing season if you so choose.

Chapter 4: Heating Your Greenhouse

For most people growing will end as temperatures start to drop, even though a greenhouse can extend the growing season by a few weeks.

To grow throughout the year or to keep frost tender plants alive over winter, you will need to heat your greenhouse. Depending on what you are growing, you may get away with just keeping the frost off, or you may need to heat the greenhouse to warmer temperatures. A heating mat may help you to germinate seeds, but plant growth is severely slowed in the colder months.

A greenhouse does help to keep your plants warmer, and it will help to keep frost away from your plants. However, if temperatures plummet too far, then no matter how well built your greenhouse, it will not keep out the frost.

Before you decide upon a heating solution for your greenhouse, you need to determine what you are growing. Different crops have different temperature requirements, and if you are growing plants that are frost hardy or tolerate cooler temperatures, then you do not need to heat your greenhouse as much.

Warmer weather crops such as tomatoes, chilies, and peppers are going to be extremely difficult to grow in a greenhouse in colder areas over winter as the heater simply will not be able to keep up. To heat your greenhouse enough, you would have to spend a fortune on heating, which would not make the investment cost-effective.

A simple, eco-friendly way to keep your greenhouse warm is to dig out a trench down the middle of your greenhouse, cover it with palettes and then make compost in it. In smaller greenhouses, this isn't going to be a huge area, but it will help to raise the temperature in your greenhouse without investing in heating equipment.

Another free heating technique is to paint some barrels, buckets, or sandbags black and leave them in your greenhouse. These will absorb heat during the day and radiate it back out at night. It isn't going to make more than a degree or two difference, but it could be enough to keep the frost off of your plants.

The easiest way to heat your greenhouse is with an electric heater, though this does require you to have electricity in your greenhouse.

Running an extension cord out isn't safe, so if you are installing electricity, then get it done professionally and safely. It has to be waterproof if it is outside, and there are likely rules and regulations in your country affecting how and where the cable can be run.

You need to ensure that your electric heat is stable and that it is away from flammable material. You also need to be cautious when watering your plants to ensure you do not damage your heater.

When using an electric heater, the air must circulate properly. This will prevent hot spots as well as cold spots and also reduce condensation. Some heaters have fans built-in, but others will need additional air circulation.

As the price of propane has been increasing, many greenhouse owners are turning to wood or pellet stoves. These are working out to be very cost-effective, even on a larger scale. You will need to check local codes and follow their requirements as well as follow common-sense safety precautions. Pellet stoves are very easy to use, often come with temperature controls, and some even have blowers that will circulate the heat.

If your greenhouse is plastic, then a wood stove is not a good idea. The stove pipe gets very hot and will melt the plastic. Ideally, your stove should be vented out through a masonry foundation or something similar rather than through glass.

Another alternative is to cover your greenhouse with plastic and line the inside with bubble wrap. This is the right solution in areas where the temperature doesn't drop too far in winter. However, in areas with several months of freezing weather, this will not keep the frost out of your greenhouse.

You can buy specific insulation for your greenhouse, which will help reduce heat loss and your heating bill. This is often put in place as the temperature drops and removed when spring has arrived.

There are propane, natural gas, petrol, and other heaters available, and these are effective. They are getting more expensive to buy, but they do a good job in a greenhouse which cannot have electricity. Many people with smaller garden greenhouses will use a propane heater. The advantage of these heaters is you do not need to have electric power in your greenhouse, meaning your greenhouse can be sited anywhere.

Heaters are rated in British Thermal Units or BTUs. The higher the BTU, then the more heat it gives out. You can calculate the number of BTU's you need for your greenhouse using formulas found online or heater suppliers will help you. You will need to take into account many factors, including the size of your greenhouse, how hot you want the greenhouse, the heat loss of the greenhouse, and more. Getting this right means, you do not waste energy heating your greenhouse or buying a heater that won't do the job.

Natural gas heaters require a gas line to be run to your greenhouse, whereas propane heaters run on gas cylinders, making them the most popular heaters with home greenhouse owners.

4.1 Where to Put Your Heater

Where you locate your heater will depend on some factors such as the location of vents and shutters, where the doors are, and more.

You need to be careful not to place your heater under a water leak or anything similar.

Depending on the floor in your greenhouse, it may be necessary to build a plinth to mount your heater on. This will ensure the heater is level and safe.

Consider all the factors, and if you are still unsure, then speak to any supplier of heaters, and they will be able to advise you.

Types of Greenhouse Heaters

There are many different types of greenhouse heater on the market, and we touched on these already. Let's go into more detail now on these different heaters together with their advantages and disadvantages.

1. Paraffin Greenhouse Heaters

Paraffin heaters are one of the most popular ways to heat a greenhouse, being both affordable and readily available. For a home gardener with a smaller greenhouse, these are ideal, but as the price of paraffin has increased in recent years, this has made these less popular.

You can buy paraffin cheaper online or in bulk, but the heaters are cheap to buy new. There is also a healthy market for used paraffin heaters, so it does make this a very affordable solution.

Paraffin heaters come in some different sizes, and in most models, the paraffin reservoir is large enough to last a day, or even two, so are low maintenance. Being self-contained, they have no requirement for electricity, and they also give off CO_2, which your plants will appreciate.

Paraffin has become less popular in recent years because of the cost of fuel, which has become harder to obtain. However, in our Internet age, it is easier now to source this fuel, though with the concerns about climate change and emissions, this type of fuel is likely to wane in popularity still further.

This type of heat is always on and is manually controlled. You can end up with the heater burning when the heat isn't needed and wasting fuel. There are no temperature controls on a paraffin heater, as it just burns. You can often adjust the size of the flame, but there is usually no way to turn off the heat when the greenhouse reaches a set temperature.

One disadvantage of paraffin heaters is that they give off water vapor, which can encourage mold if the greenhouse isn't suitably ventilated.

2. Electric Greenhouse Heaters

These are a great form of heating, but it does require your greenhouse to have an electricity supply. Electric heaters are controlled by a thermostat, so you have greater control over the heat output and, therefore, over your running costs.

To avoid the dangers of mixing water with electricity, you have to make sure you get a heater designed to work in a greenhouse and that the electricity supply is safe and protected from water and damp.

Electric heaters are not for everyone because of the cost of running electrical cables to a greenhouse. If you are on an allotment site, then you are very unlikely to have access to electricity. Depending on local regulations, you may need to hire a professional to lay the cable and use armored cable.

The advantage of an electric fan heater is that it does circulate air around the greenhouse, which avoids hot and cold spots. This also helps to reduce the risk of fungal problems from poor air circulation.

3. Propane Gas Heaters

Run from propane bottles, these are relatively cheap to run, and propane can be refilled at many camping stores or gas stations. For a greenhouse without electricity, these are a viable solution.

You will need to ensure your greenhouse is well ventilated because propane gas heaters produce water vapor. They also produce CO_2, which your plants will appreciate.

Many propane heaters come with thermostatic controls, which gives you a degree of control over your running costs.

4.2 Mains Gas Heating

This is an excellent method of heating larger greenhouses. The installation costs are high, but the running costs are reasonable.

You will need a natural gas pipe run to your greenhouse. Again this is not for everyone, and in most cases, natural gas is not going to be a cost-effective form of heating your greenhouse.

This is most popular with commercial growers in large greenhouses and isn't something most home growers will install.

4.3 Greenhouse Heating Tips

Obviously, you want to keep your heating costs down during winter while keeping your plants warm and alive. Here are some of my favorite tips to effectively and efficiently heat your greenhouse:

- **Bubble Wrap Is Your Friend** – clip bubble wrap to the inside of your greenhouse frame to help reduce heat loss and block draughts. You can buy horticultural bubble wrap, which is both toughened and UV stabilized. Remember that larger bubbles will let lighter get into your greenhouse to your plants. This bubble wrap can also be used on tender outdoor plants and pots to protect them from frost.

- **Don't Be Afraid of the Thermostat** – if your heater has a thermostat, then use it! You can set your heater only to come on when temperatures go below a certain point. You may need to experiment with the temperature a little so that the heat kicks in and heats your greenhouse before the plants get too cold.

- **Choose The Right Temperature** – most plants are not going to appreciate a tropical jungle temperature, so if you are just preventing frost, all you need to do is keep your greenhouse at 2C/36F. Some tender plants, including citrus trees, prefer a higher minimum temperature of 7C/45F as will many young plants. Delicate plants will require higher temperatures, depending on the plant.

- **Buy A Thermometer** – a good thermometer that can record maximum and minimum temperatures is going to help you a lot with your greenhouse. By knowing how low the temperature drops at night, you will be able to use your heater more efficiently and save yourself some money. It also helps you understand how hot your greenhouse gets during the day, so you know whether or not you need to cool it down.

- **Think About Heater Position** – where you locate the heaters will influence how well your greenhouse is heated. Electric heaters are positioned away from water, and so it circulates the air around the greenhouse. With all heaters, you need to be careful that they don't point directly at plants and dry out the leaves.

- **Heat What You Need to** – heating a greenhouse can be expensive, so if you only have a few delicate plants, then put them in one place, surround them with a bubble wrap or Perspex curtain, and then heat just that area. There is no point you spending money heating a greenhouse that is mostly empty when all you need to do is warm up a small area.

- **Use Horticultural Fleece** – on the coldest nights, a couple of layers of this will give your plants that extra bit of protection by raising their Temperature a few vital degrees. Remember, though, to remove the fleece during the day, so the plants are well ventilated and don't overheat.

- **Ventilate** – heating your greenhouse increases humidity, so it is vital that you have proper ventilation. This will keep your greenhouse healthy and prevent the build-up of fungal diseases.

- **Water Early On** – you can help reduce the humidity in your greenhouse by watering your plants earlier on in the day. Irrigate the plants the water they need and try not to overwater or water the floor in your greenhouse unless you are damping down.

- **Use Your Vents Wisely** – open your greenhouse vents early in the morning on sunny days to clear condensation. Close them before the sun goes down, so you trap the warmth of the day in the greenhouse. This will help your heaters to be more efficient.

- **Use a Heated Propagator** – if you are germinating seeds in your greenhouse, you do not need to heat the entire greenhouse unless you are starting off a lot of seeds. A heated propagation mat will help keep your seeds and seedlings warm without the expense of heating the whole greenhouse.

Depending on what you are growing and how much you want to extend your growing season, you may want to heat your greenhouse. For many people, though, the cost is high, and it isn't practical to do so. Small paraffin or propane heater, though, can be enough to keep the frost out of your greenhouse, extending the growing season enough, so your tomatoes, peppers, and chilies have time to ripen fully!

Chapter 5: Greenhouse Problems

5.1 Potential Greenhouse Problems

The greenhouse provides a perfect breeding ground for many diseases and pests. Many can be avoided by growing cops to be robust enough to deal with most problems, but some insects and diseases will need to be managed. You can do a lot to stop them from taking over of pests and diseases. Maintain as clean and uncluttered as possible the growing environment, clearing rubbish and washing and sterilizing used pots. Wash the insides with a garden disinfectant and scrub all the surfaces, including the road, benches, and frame; in the winter, clear the greenhouse and give it a thorough cleaning.

Clear any algae stuck inside glass overlaps and clean up an aluminum frame's uncomfortable moldings. Inspect them for signs of insect attack and disease attack when you carry plants back inside. When sowing and planting, always use sterilized pots and compost soil mix. If you buy plants, make sure they're free from pests and diseases, so they don't put in your greenhouse problems. Make sure you allow your plants to be in the right environment so that they grow rapidly and do not experience growth control.

Use your watering time to closely inspect plants, especially the growing tips and undersides of leaves, for any early insect or disease symptoms activity, and take prompt action when needed. You should be able to avoid using chemical controls if you are vigilant. By covering vents with insect-proof mesh, some infestations can be prevented. You are using sticky traps, which consist of sheets of yellow plastic coated with non-drying glue if insects are in the greenhouse. For a wide range of flying pests, this method of non-chemical control is becoming common and works particularly well in a greenhouse.

If there is a serious pest or disease attack, make sure that you select the right chemical for the problem and follow the instructions given on the label by the manufacturer. During heat, capillary matting is an ideal way to cool the majority of pot plants. You can use a proprietary mains water-fed system or improvise with a system like the one in the mall that uses a gutter length to supply water. With special water bags or from a cistern, you can keep it topped by hand. This is the exact system and steps to avoid greenhouse gardening problems.

5.2 The Most Common Greenhouse Mistake

If you've been gardening for any amount of time, you either needed a greenhouse or wondered if it would be beneficial for you to get a greenhouse, most of us get on the internet and start researching all the things we need to consider; the climate we're living in, ventilation, what we're going to grow and when; racks and shelves, etc., etc.

If we decide, we'll get a greenhouse and get all we can dream of! We calculate and test where the sun is going to be and then begin to look for our buck's best bang. This is where most of us make a mistake that, in a very short time, will come back to haunt us; we buy a greenhouse that ends up being too small.

You may think that it's the money that makes the difference, but it's not at all. In the growing house, we underestimate what can be done and end up with more plans and plants than space! Then we are forced to go back and buy a second greenhouse to either add or replace the first. The problem is that you go a bit blind into the greenhouse experience if you don't practice exactly what you'd like to do.

Consider lots of things before your new greenhouse that can help you determine the best size about how your garden and what your purpose is. If you're the type of experimenter, just save the trouble and buy one to two sizes larger than you think you need because you're going to use your greenhouse on a year-round basis for a lot of things.

If you're the guy who loves to be out in the yard, even if it's a bit chilly or windy, and your wife thinks you're nuts, buy one size bigger than you think you should. If you're just planting to grow some vegetables and hoping to do the same; just make sure you get a greenhouse with a good insulation ratio for longer or year-round, and you'll need to find out what kinds of vegetables and herbs you're planning to grow and make sure you've got enough expansion room to grow all you want in the winter dead. Once, buy more than you think you need at least one amount.

Choose one size more than you think you need unless you just want to putter around and play with growing in a greenhouse. In other words, buy more than you think you need at least one number. It will save you time, money, and frustration in the long run.

Chapter 6: Buying a Used Greenhouse

Buying a new greenhouse is just too expensive for many. They aren't cheap, and the cost means many people do not buy one.

A good option is to buy a used greenhouse either through eBay, Freecycle, Gumtree, or local ads. Often these are a fraction of the price of a new greenhouse, and you can even find greenhouses for free! Some people, when they move into a new home, find a greenhouse they don't want and will offer it for free to someone who is willing to come and take it away.

When buying a used greenhouse, you will be expected in many cases to disassemble the greenhouse yourself. Take lots of pictures of the greenhouse before you take it apart, as it will help you to put it back together again. Make notes on any non-standard panes and where they belong. Plenty of pictures from all angles is the easiest way to do this.

Taking a greenhouse down and reassembling it will be a two-person job, so you need to find yourself a helper to make the job easier.

You will need some tools to take down the greenhouse, including a wide selection of spanners, both open and closed-ended. You will also need a variety of screwdrivers, both flat and cross-head, and also large ones. A ratchet spanner will help you a lot and make things easier. A good pair of pliers can also help with the more stubborn bolts.

I would also recommend a can of WD-40 to help ease rusted bolts as well as a junior hacksaw for those exceptionally stubborn bolts.

You should wear gloves, particularly while moving the glass; otherwise, you will end up with plenty of cuts on your hands.

Ideally, you will want to disassemble the greenhouse on a dry day because doing it in the rain is unpleasant (trust me on this) and much harder as everything becomes slippery.

It is worthwhile labeling parts as you take them apart as it will help you a lot when putting it back together. If you can get a van, then you don't have to take the greenhouse down completely. You can just break it into the front, rear, and side panels and the two halves of the roof and fit them in the van. It will save you a *lot* of work if you can do it this way!

Most used greenhouses will be on the smaller side, usually 8x6' or thereabouts. If you want a larger greenhouse, then just get two smaller greenhouses and join them together!

As with any greenhouse, the first thing you need to do is build a base following instructions. Just make sure that the base is square (measure the diagonals) and level (use a spirit level that is at least 3 feet long).

Before you dive headlong into assembling your greenhouse, you need to sort out all the bits and pieces. Make sure you have enough nuts and bolts and that those you have are usable. Sometimes they can be rusted, or the thread stripped, so you will want to have enough to hand. The last thing you want is to be halfway through when you discover you are missing vital parts. Buy these from most home improvement stores or online.

Also, make sure you have plenty of glass clips as these often go missing or get broken when taking a greenhouse to pieces.

Make sure all the glass pieces are present, and none are broken. You cannot assemble your greenhouse without all the panes, as that will make it extremely susceptible to wind damage.

Check the weather forecast before you start building your greenhouse as doing it in the rain is no fun and doing it in high winds is positively dangerous!

Sort the struts out, group them together into each of the sides and the roof. This allows you to check you have all the pieces and then assemble each side before you put it all together.

Once the frame is assembled, you need to start putting the glass in place. This is best done from the top down because you can get around the greenhouse better without glass in the frame beneath you. This is when you realize that your glazing clips are broken, twisted, or even missing, so buy a bag or two before you start! Remember that glass doesn't bend, so you need to be careful putting it in. An 8x6' greenhouse can end up using up to 200 of these clips!

It is also worthwhile buying some extra rubber seals that the glass fits into. Invariably when taking a greenhouse to pieces, these will break or get lost.

Buy all the spare parts you need before you start reassembling the greenhouse. It will make your life much easier.

Just remember to be careful when reassembling your greenhouse. The glass can and will break, so transport it with care. It isn't a race, so just take your time and make sure you have someone to help you!

Chapter 7: Greenhouse Irrigation Systems

7.1 Different Irrigation Systems in Greenhouses

Your greenhouse may have the best climate control system and rich mix of rot for each plant, but your irrigation system is one of the most important elements for growing flowers, leaves and plants, and healthy fruits. Although you can get away with manual watering with a well of water, using the right method of greenhouse irrigation saves time. The effectiveness of each method depends on the size of the greenhouse.

The system of irrigation for the crop greenhouse includes the following:

- Manual irrigation
- Perimeter irrigation system
- Tube sprinkler system
- Irrigation system for drops
- Height spray system
- Flow and reflux system.
- **Manual watering**

This is the most common sprinkler system, but less expensive and more expensive, but still used when on hand - with labor, it is inexpensive, and the scale of operation is quite small, and automation is not practical. Hand water requires considerable time and is not a pleasant job. But it is always followed when crops are of high density, such as the production of food, shrimp, or pot.

When manual irrigation is practiced, care should be taken to ensure that the strength of the water dissociates, either by using a fine-rose spray or by grinding at the end of the pipe, to avoid washing the root substrate with jars or curves and interrupting the root structure.

- **Perimeter irrigation system**

In this system, the pipes cross the perimeters of a bank with an object that squeezes the surface of the water root under the foliage. Therefore, this system is most relevant to the production of fresh flowers. The tubes can be galvanized iron or PVC can be fixed. In these pipes, the nozzles are mounted at an angle of 45, 90, or 180 degrees. Normally, 19 mm diameter tubes are used. Depending on the length of the beds, a valve can be supplied later.

- **Tube sprinkler system**

This system is mainly used for water jars. The polyethylene microtube carries water to each pot. These microtubes are available in various internal diameters ranging from 0.9, 1.1, 1.3, 1.5, 1.9 mm, and more.

The number of jars that can be irrigated by a 19 mm main water pipe depends on the internal diameter of the microtube used. For example, a 0.9, 1.1, 1.3, 1.5 mm microtube can process 600, 900, 700, and 400 vessels, respectively. These microtubes will have to weigh at the end so that the speed of the water can break; otherwise, the pipe could be blown out of the well and dig a small hole in the media.

- **Drip irrigation system**

This system is ideal for greenhouse cultivation. There is a water-saving of 50 to 70% compared to the conventional irrigation system. It allows the even distribution of water, nutrients, pesticides, and fungicides without waste.

The drip irrigation system supplies water to crops through a network of main, secondary, and lateral lines with an emission point spaced at regular intervals over the long term. Each diver or transmitter provides a uniform, measured, and controlled application of water, nutrients, pesticides, fungicides, and growth substances directly into the root zone of the plant.

Water and nutrients enter the earth through emitters that move toward the root zone of plants under the combined effect of gravity and capillary forces. In this way, plants immediately acquire moisture and nutrients, which guarantees that plants never suffer from water stress, thus improving their quality. It results in excellent growth and high efficiency.

PVC pipes are used for the distribution of water from the main source to the underlines. Drops from 12-16 mm droplets are securely placed in each row of plants directly connected to the underlines. The emitters installed in the flanges are located just next to the plant for a gradual distribution of water to the root of the plants.

Pipes should be maintained regularly by adding chlorine or other chemicals to the drift tube to kill bacteria and algae. Acid treatment is also needed to dissolve calcium carbonate. Precautions should be taken against rodents to avoid damaging pipes. Look carefully for leakage hoses, which should be done regularly.

- **Height spray system**

Greenhouse crops are the easiest and least expensive crops that can be irrigated from above. In this system, the tubes are suspended from the floor from 60 cm to 180 cm. The nuts are mounted in the tubes at 360 °. It will ensure that the water is of good quality and is properly filtered so that these nuts do not get wet.

- **Flow and reflux system**

This is a secondary irrigation system for plant plants and beds. The pots or dishes are grown on a plastic or glass level bench available in different widths (1.2 to 2.0 m) and whose length is 1 m. These banks are glued together to form a bank of the desired width. These banks can go for support. These have channels for draining irrigation water.

There is a water tank under the bank. This tank is covered to prevent the growth of dust or algae. For water from the well, the water stays in the bank for 10 minutes and is collected in a cistern and reused. Fertilizers can also be applied through this irrigation system. The pin with the bottom arm is better than the side holes.

7.2 Advantages of the Greenhouse Irrigation System

All modern irrigation systems are useful in different ways, depending on their use. Here are some of the reasons why you should consider installing a greenhouse irrigation system.

Filtration systems

Most greenhouse irrigation systems use filters to prevent the flow path encroachment of small emitters from small particles suspended in the water. New technologies are introduced to reduce obstruction. Some domestic systems are introduced without additional filters because the drinking water is already filtered into the water treatment plant.

Almost all greenhouse equipment companies suggest using filters in a system. Due to sediment collapse and accidental insertion of particles into intermediate tubes, it is advisable to use the latest pipe filters just before the last discharge pipe, in addition to the other filters in the pipe.

Water conservation

Greenhouse irrigation can guarantee water conservation by reducing evaporation and deep drainage compared to different irrigation methods, such as flood irrigation, because water can be applied, more precisely, at the roots of plants

In addition, the drop can eliminate many diseases that spread by contact with the foliage. In areas where groundwater is limited, there may not be real water savings, but in desert areas or in sandy soils, the system will provide drop irrigation flows.

Factors of work and efficiency

Drip irrigation works by water moving slowly and directly to the root of the plant. Just apply water where needed, for example, at the roots of the plant instead of everywhere. Drip systems are simple and relatively insensitive to design and installation errors.

It is a very effective method for water plants. For example, the standard sprinkler system has an efficiency of about 75 to 85%. In contrast, a greenhouse irrigation system has an efficiency level of more than 90%. But over time, this difference in terms of water supply and efficiency will make a real difference in terms of the quality and profitability of the plant.

As expected, in areas where water resources are scarce, such as desert areas around the world, the greenhouse irrigation system has become the preferred method of irrigation. They are relatively inexpensive and easy to install, simple in design, and help maximize the health of plants for optimum moisture levels.

Profit

Irrigation systems are essential in modern agriculture because they greatly improve agricultural production. A greenhouse irrigation system may seem expensive in the short term, but it will save money and efforts in the long run. For example, this system can contribute to reducing the cost of production by at least 30% by controlling the amount of water, agrochemicals, and labor costs - to implement. However, it is advisable to have a quality greenhouse irrigation system that offers significant benefits

7.3 Grow Stronger Plants with a Good Greenhouse Watering System

There are many different types of greenhouse irrigation systems, but the most common system is the micro irrigation method or more commonly called a drip irrigation system. Tests have shown that using an irrigation system properly can improve your plant growth by up to 70%.

Watering the plants is a mistake much make because it is really difficult to judge how much water the plants need. Plants can cause them to rot over-irrigation, get fungal infections, and die. Similarly, underwater it is very easy to dry out the soil and wilt the plants. I'd suggest that you invest in a watering system once you've built your greenhouse. And better still, while it is being installed, because at this point, it is much easier to install the pipework than later.

Low maintenance extremely handy is a strong irrigation system. You won't have to walk twice a day down to the greenhouse to do the watering. A proper system, designed properly, will provide you with very little maintenance and maintenance for many years of service.

Drip irrigation slowly affects the roots of your plants and vegetables with a flow of water. There is very little waste or evaporation as the water gets straight to the soil's roots. This is suitable regardless of the climate in which you are, as you do not need to consider sun and wind evaporation.

Improve Plant Production & Efficiency The most common practice for small greenhouses is to water the greenhouse by hand. If you have a bigger greenhouse or are interested in taking a more professional approach, I would recommend that you get an automated system. This is an ideal way to increase your production and maintain an efficient business. In the long run, this will not only save you time, but you will also save money.

You may think that hand watering is a low-cost alternative to paying for automated equipment. Yet our experiments have shown that watering plants correctly and uniformly recover the price of equipment. You can never be sure when watering by hand, which plants were overlooked, and which plants were saturated. It is easy to avoid the price of replacing damaged plants by automating the cycle from the start.

Offset Labor Costs If you are running a growing professional business or perhaps thinking about starting one up, then you have to consider the labor costs. An effective greenhouse watering system is relatively easy to install and will cost much less to operate than the amount you'll have to shell out for a season in labor. Prices will vary depending on the region size and the variety of plants being cultivated. Many plants will need more regular watering. Some of them are less common, but with more water. If you water hanging baskets or containers of small size, the best choice is to drip irrigation. When you deal with larger containers, however, it might be worth looking like an option into a spray device.

Chapter 8: Pests and Diseases

8.1 Pests and Disease Control

One of the major problems many greenhouse farmers face is controlling pests and diseases in their gardens. Pests and diseases can affect plant production, so knowing how to manage these pests and control the spread of diseases can help for a more profitable farm.

8.2 Pest Management

Pests are any unwanted organisms in the greenhouse. Pests can affect the normal functioning of plants, and they include weeds, algae, spider mites, insects, and any other organism that can damage plants in the greenhouse.

Many farmers come up with an integrated pest management program to help them solve the problems they have on their farms. Coming up with an integrated disease management system will enable you to identify a wide range of measures you can use to control and prevent all types of diseases.

For any prevention measures to take place, you need to identify the potential infection to the crops. Doing this step will minimize the risk of infection and reduce the spread of the disease to other crops.

Integrated pest management involves coming up with a set of practices to manage and control pests. Controlling pests on the farm will enable you to have healthy and productive crops. Pests and diseases can affect the normal functioning and development of the crop, so controlling these pests and diseases will make the crop more productive.

Conditions Necessary for Disease Occurrence

- Presence of a pathogen.
- Favorable environmental conditions for the pathogen to survive.
- Plant susceptibility to the disease.

In the disease and pest control triangle, if you can control one or more of these conditions, you are a step closer to controlling the pest (pathogen).

You can control pests on the farm either through the use of pesticides or maintaining good hygiene on the farm. Changing the environmental conditions, so they are unfavorable to the pathogen will limit its growth. You can also plant pest-resistant crops on the farm.

8.3 Maintaining Greenhouse Hygiene

Maintaining the hygiene of the greenhouse is one of the most effective methods you can use to keep pathogens at bay. All the containers, pots, materials, and any other equipment brought inside the greenhouse should be clean.

Installing a foot bath is also essential, especially when dealing with a commercial greenhouse. You should maintain the foot bath and change the disinfectant solution often, as this will minimize the risk of pathogens into the greenhouse.

Alternatively, you can empty the greenhouse and thoroughly clean it as you prepare for the fall season or between crops. Full cleaning of the structure helps remove any pathogens and diseases in the soil compost.

8.4 Use Disease-Free Plants

One source of pests is through contaminated seeds. Always buy seeds from trusted sources to avoid bringing pests to your farm through this medium.

When buying seedlings for transplant in your garden, inspect them upon delivery. If you are satisfied and they are disease-free, you can take them inside your greenhouse. Always make sure the storage area is clean and store the seedlings as they await a transplant.

If any of the delivered seedlings looks infected, put it in a sealed plastic bag and take it for further testing. Do not plant any infected or potentially infected plants to avoid a spread of pests and diseases to the rest in your greenhouse.

You should also plant pest-resistant crops. Most crops are tolerant to downy mildew and powdery mildew diseases.

8.5 Control the Growing Environment

Making the conditions unfavorable for the pest to survive in the greenhouse environment is the most effective method of pest control. Controlling the Temperature and humidity limits the replication of diseases in the greenhouse.

Monitor the plants regularly to identify any early infection of the plants. This will enable you to take control measures before the pathogens completely damage the plant or spread across the entire greenhouse.

You should throw away pruned material or any other crop residual. Don't leave them to pile in the greenhouse — put all pruned material into disposal bags and throw them out, away from the greenhouse, to avoid creating a breeding environment for pathogens. Immediately bury any crop debris from the greenhouse.

Remove weeds growing inside and outside the greenhouse, as weeds can provide a breeding place for pests, insects, and diseases. Removing weeds will help control insects that carry diseases into your plants.

8.6 Control Entry to the Greenhouse

You will find most greenhouse pests near doorways, as people can carry these pests and pathogens with them on their clothes and shoes while they walk around. Limit access to the greenhouse, so only a few people can enter.

If there are people visiting your greenhouse, give them disposable overalls to wear and let them pass through the installed foot bath. Avoid inviting visitors coming directly from other farms into your own farm because they may carry a lot of pathogens from their farm and bring them to yours.

Visitors should move from the young and healthy plants in the greenhouse to the older plants. This reduces the risk of spreading pathogens through the greenhouse.

8.7 Tips for Pest and Disease Control

1. Determine the Vulnerability of the Plants

Monitor your crops to know when they are vulnerable to pathogens. For example, bacterial diseases affect crops when their leaves sprout out, but they are less likely to affect the plant after the latter's maturity or propagation stage. Crops are also vulnerable to diseases when in the storage room, waiting to be shipped.

2. **Determine Which Biocontrol Agents are Suitable for Your Farm**

You should know the best bio control agent to use for all your gardening operations. Different biocontrol agents affect pests in different ways; therefore, choosing the best biological control will help you control the pests in your garden.

3. **Sanitation of the Greenhouse**

You should prioritize your greenhouse's sanitation as a defense mechanism against all pests and pathogens. Sanitation involves cleaning the structure to avoid the spread of diseases, removing all plant debris, and weeding the inside and outside of the structure.

4. **Choose the Right Insecticide.**

There are different types of insecticides used for pest management. Before choosing which type of insecticide to use, determine the common pest problems you face in the greenhouse when you harvest, and your ultimate plant produces a goal. This will help you choose the correct insecticide for your needs.

5. **Establish Consistency in Pest Control**

Be consistent in pest control measures, as this will lead to a reduced cost for maintaining the greenhouse. It also ensures you can keep an ideal temperature and humidity within the structure.

8.8 Integrated Pest Management Techniques

Integrated pest management includes a systematic approach to solving pest issues on the farm. It provides long-term prevention mechanisms and control measures for handling pests and other pathogens on the farm.

These approaches include:

- Monitoring pest infestation.
- Identifying the types of pests on the farm.
- Coming up with control measures.
  - Biological control
  - Chemical control
  - Sanitation
  - Mechanical control measures
- Follow up/evaluation.

- **Monitoring Pest Infestation**

This step involves assessing the pest infestation on the farm. It also determines potential pest infestations on your plants. Always do a thorough assessment each day to determine the status of the crops based on their appearance. Keep note of the appearance of the plant and any slight change, and you should also know the signs or symptoms of various potential pests. Daily monitoring of the plants is the key to coming up with early prevention measures.

8.9 Identify the Type of Pests Affecting the Crops

When pests infest crops, they damage the normal functioning of the crop. Similar to weeds, pests inside the greenhouse compete with the plants for water, light, and nutrients. Different pests affect plants differently; therefore, the plant damage or injury will depend on the type of pest-infested in the plant. These pests can include:

1. **Insects and Spiders**

Insects eat on the plant leaves and other parts of the plant. They also nest on the plants' parts and are often invisible. It's important to know how each pest affects the plant to know which signs to look for in determining the type of pest you are dealing with.

2. **Diseases**

Some common diseases affecting plants in the greenhouse include fungi, viruses, and bacteria.

3. **Environmental Conditions**

Some environmental conditions are favorable to the growth and spread of pathogens within the greenhouse, and different environmental conditions encourage different pest infestations in the greenhouse. Some conditions include:

- Little or too much water.
- Little or too much light.
- Nutrient deficiency in the soil and phytotoxicities.

4. **Weeds**

The presence of weeds in the greenhouse will cause deficiencies in the crops sown. It competes for nutrients with the crops, limiting the number of nutrients a plant needs to grow.

Weeds also provide a conducive environment for breeding pests. Always come up with consistent weed control and prevention mechanisms in the greenhouse. Weeds such as prostrate spurge and woodsorrel affect plant produce.

5. **Algae**

This is dangerous that affects the people working in the greenhouse; however, it doesn't have any effect on the crops.

6. Snails and Slugs

Snails and slugs affect the younger crops in the greenhouse, and they eat the soft parts of the plants.

7. Nematodes

Nematodes affect the roots of the plant, as they make the roots of the crop swell and knot.

8.10 Control Measures

After monitoring the crops and identifying pests affecting them, the next step is to come up with control measures to solve these issues. You can take action that is: biological, chemical, mechanical, or with sanitation processes.

Biocontrol Measures/Biological Controls

Biocontrol measures rely on the use of biological agents to control the growth of pests in the greenhouse. These agents are safer than chemical agents, and they include plants, animals, and microbes.

They have some beneficial organisms, such as predatory insects and microorganisms, and fungi, and you can use any of these predators to control pests in the greenhouse. Biocontrol has less of an impact on the environment.

Chemical Control Measures

This method uses products with chemicals such as pesticides and insecticides to control pests. There are two types of pesticides: those labeled for general use and those labeled for restricted use.

You can buy the general use of pesticides at any garden retail center, and they will be safe to use within your greenhouse. Restricted use pesticides are restricted to use under the supervision of a certified applicator. Its uses are also restricted.

Mechanical Control Measures

Mechanical control processes use hands-on and exclusion methods to control pests; that is, handpicking and destroying the pests in the greenhouse.

Exclusion processes involve closing the doors to ensure pests don't enter inside the greenhouse.

Cultural/Sanitation Processes

Sanitation methods of pest control ensure the environmental conditions are unfavorable for the breeding of pests. Having a well-organized, clean, and the sanitized environment is an effective way of managing pests. Ensure there is proper temperature control measures, a watering system, and good fertilization of plants.

8.11 Disease Preventive Measures

To control diseases in the greenhouse, you need proper sanitation and a keen eye. Pay a lot of attention to the growth of the crops and note down any slight change. You may have health problems and sudden bacteria growing inside from air infecting the plants. Without preventing measures and preparation, even the tiniest disease can cause huge damage to the crops.

It is not easy to get rid of fungus and bacteria that are affecting your crops quickly, but you can minimize the risk the bacteria will have in your greenhouse.

You can minimize the risk through:

- Proper sanitization of containers, potting media, shelves, stands, and any other tools you use inside the greenhouse.
- Clean the greenhouse surfaces regularly. This can help prevent spore germination in the structure.
- Monitor the temperatures and humidity inside and ensure

the greenhouse environment is not prone to disease.
- Ensure there is proper ventilation by increasing the supply of fresh air circulation inside.
- Make sure there is enough space between the plants to increase air circulation around them.
- Avoid water splashing on your plants; only water them at the base or on their crowns.
- Monitor new seedlings to ensure they are disease-free.
- Check the crops daily for any signs of disease, discolorations, or any other symptoms.

8.12 Common Greenhouse Diseases

There are various common diseases you may come across while tending to your garden. Some of the sources include infected plants from outside, carried in by insects, or floating in the air. The following sections will outline some of these diseases in more detail.

Fungus

Wet conditions or overwatering can cause fungus diseases like phytophthora, powdery mildew, root rot, and botrytis. You should monitor the moisture and humidity level in the greenhouse to avoid conditions that favor the breeding of fungus.

Ensure there is proper drainage of containers and other potting media and do not leave plants soaked in water for a long time.

When fungi infect plants, the plants start to wilt and discolor. Sometimes, they may have fuzzy growth on their stem and leaves, which may later turn yellow in color.

If the infections affect only the surface of the plant, you can apply neem oil and increase air circulation in the area. If the fungi affect the plant tissue, you should remove the plants from your garden and discard them far away. It is difficult to treat tissue-affected plants.

Bacterial Diseases

Some bacterial diseases that affect plants include Erwinia and bacterial blight. It is not easy to cure these diseases, and if they infect your plants, you will have to get them out of the garden and destroy them immediately.

The infected plants will have water-soaked spots while its tissue melts into a sticky mess. If you notice any of these signs, remove them right away.

Bacterial diseases can spread to other plants through dirty tools, potting medium, and containers. Proper sanitation and increased air circulation are important factors in preventing the spread of bacterial diseases.

Viruses

Viruses occur in various forms and sizes and are brought inside the greenhouse by insects (thrips and aphids), which are classified as plant-feeding insects. Plants infected by a virus have a yellow color or mosaic patterns on their leaves. If you notice any signs of a virus infection on your plants, you should take them out and destroy them immediately.

Always monitor your greenhouse for insects and treat your plants when they appear as soon as possible.

For any pest and disease control mechanisms to succeed, you must:

- Understand the various components of greenhouse diseases.
- Understand the different sources of the diseases you're facing; that is, are they caused by organisms or influenced

by the conditions in the greenhouse?

- Understand the different symptoms of all the pathogens. Know signs of root rot, symptoms of bacteria and virus affected plants, and those of mildews, as knowing them will help you decide which pesticide or control mechanism to apply.
- Know the resistance mechanisms of the pests and fungi.

To control root rots in the greenhouse, you need to:

- Remove the infected crops.
- Sterilize the potting media.
- Wash your hands with soap to avoid spreading pathogens to other areas.
- Control the irrigation system to have moderate soil moisture. The potting medium used should have adequate drainage to avoid waterlogged crops, and you should also make sure you are not overwatering the crops.
- Use the right fungicides to prevent seedling infections.

You would control powdery mildew pests by:

- Reducing the greenhouse's humidity.
- Removing dead plant debris or material.
- Using fungicides to prevent the spread of infections.

If the irrigation water is the one causing pathogens, you should decontaminate the water through chemical treatment, filtration, or an irradiation method.

Chapter 9: Build a Solid Foundation

9.1 Choosing the Correct Foundation

Your foundation is a critical component of the greenhouse. It must be able to serve a few specific functions, including a solid structural base, a stable and washable surface, and a material that can help to retain heat.

While greenhouses can incorporate dirt as the foundation, such as simple greenhouse tunnels or cold frames, most hold strong with the help of concrete or solid brick. Concrete and brick foundations allow heat to be absorbed and released slowly long after the sun goes down. It also provides a surface that can support tables, heavy potted plants, structural components, and can serve to protect other systems like electrical and plumbing.

Since water is a major component of successful plant growth, you can expect a few spills here and there. Dirt or other loose-fill substrates may contribute to muddy, sloppy surfaces that can become unstable or promote unwanted plant life in your greenhouse, concrete, and brick help to prevent these issues and provide an easy-to-clean surface. If you have a small space or pop-up greenhouse, you can position it on a concrete patio. If no concrete is available, you may be able to substitute with a similar product, like concrete masonry blocks (CMU), asphaltic roofing, or a similar impermeable barrier. Regardless of what you choose, keep in mind that you will want a water-resistant surface that is stable and helps to prevent unwanted plant growth at the ground level.

9.2 Preparing the Site for a Greenhouse

To prepare your site, you'll need a fairly level tract of land or pad, to begin with. This will help to limit the amount of work when developing the greenhouse. The slope and grade will play a key role in water runoff, along with orientation and access.

All plants and vegetation will need to be cleared in advance of the initial work. If you are putting the greenhouse in a vacant lot, you'll need to make sure to provide access for vehicles or equipment and pay close attention to access limitations. You'll also want to consider the damage that could be caused to existing landscaping as a result of tires, heavy equipment, and general traffic. Fences or obstructions may need to be removed.

When the site is cleared and ready for initial dirt work, you can begin with pulling sod and grading the earth to a level starting point. This will require that you call to mark out potential utilities that might be buried below ground. If you intend to frame up an above-ground pad that doesn't require digging, you may still want to confirm if utilities exist beneath the structure for future reference.

Once these initial elements are cleared out, you can start to stake out the ground and run a string level at all corners or the perimeter. This will help to determine the initial level surface so you can cut out or fill as needed. To find the level point, string a line between one stake and another, and use a line level to adjust the height.

Continue this process around the perimeter and make adjustments as you go. You may need to raise or lower your line to complete the task properly.

Once your line is level, consider which direction you'll want the water to flow off the surface of the floor and off of the roof. Improper water drainage can erode surfaces and cause damage to the foundation. Pooling water inside the greenhouse can create slip hazards. Make sure your water has a path out of the structure and away from the structure.

9.3 Top-Notch Materials for the Best Foundation

Once your base is level, you can choose what kind of materials to incorporate into the foundation. The best way to secure a solid, stable foundation is to start with a layer of aggregate (rock) of a type that tends to lock together when under pressure. River rock is rounded and moves easily compared to fractured rock that locks itself into place.

Once you have a solid base of aggregate, add a fine layer of sand and put it into place. The sand will help to bind larger aggregate into place like mortar on a brick wall. It will also help to prevent weed growth.

At the surface of the rock and sand layer, you may want to include a vapor barrier. This will help to prevent moisture from wicking up from the soil below, and it can help to prevent destructive plant growth in your foundation. Keep in mind that a greenhouse will provide an ideal location for plants to thrive, and if they find a way to grow, the roots may cause damage to your foundation.

9.4 Taking Steps to a Solid Foundation

The next step for your foundation will depend on what materials you choose. If your plan is to incorporate brick, you may be able to add another layer of finer sand and start mapping out your brick pattern right away.

If you choose a concrete foundation, you'll want to set up a rebar in the appropriate grid pattern required for the size of your pad. Concrete forms will be required around the perimeter to hold the concrete and rock substrate. This may require permitting and inspections before you can proceed to lay concrete.

Depending on the scale of your greenhouse, you might prefer to mix and spread your own concrete. However, it may be far more than you can accomplish on your own in a reasonable timeframe and skill level. You may want to consider contracting the concrete work out or calling in a concrete delivery truck to reduce the amount of hand-mixing and spreading. Be sure to consider this in your budget and call to determine the costs of delivery and scheduling.

Your concrete forms and the grade of sand and rock will help to keep your concrete costs low. They'll also help to prevent cracks over time and allow for proper curing. The concrete pour will need to be properly finished and sloped for water drainage. In addition, you'll want to make sure to allow the concrete to cure. This means it will need to harden as it dries, adding strength and integrity. Cold, wet environments can hinder proper curing, so the schedule works during stable, dry periods.

Brick floors have no dry time but will require special care with regard to cavities between bricks. Fine sand will help to prevent movement between bricks. Once you have your brick pattern laid out, you can sweep fine sand or powder between the cracks. This will help lock the bricks into place. A solid perimeter around all sides will also help keep brick contained.

Chapter 10: Starting Seeds

One of the best ways to get the plants to grow in your greenhouses is by planting seeds. Seeds are available to buy at a very low price point when compared to buying entire plants. They are also rewarding. When you decide to plant a seed, and then it sprouts, you get the satisfaction of helping that tiny seed to turn into something great. Seeds are a great thing to plant inside of your greenhouse.

There are two different reasons why you would want to plant seeds in your greenhouse. The first of these reasons is that you are wanting to get a head start on growing plants that can be transplanted into your outdoor garden once the weather is nice enough.

If you want to start seeds to transplant into your outdoor garden, you will want to start them in your greenhouse so that they are able to grow when the weather is still too cold for them to grow outside. Typically, you are going to want to plant your seeds about six weeks before the last estimated frost date in your area. However, if you start your seeds in the greenhouse, your plants will be mature and ready to go by the time that the last frost happens. This will make your harvest be able to happen earlier, and it will increase the odds of your plants surviving outside since they already got a good strong start in your perfect greenhouse environment.

The other way that you can start seeds in a greenhouse is if you want them to live in your greenhouse for their entire life span. In this method, you would start your seeds in your greenhouse in you would keep the plants in your greenhouse all the way through harvest time. If you choose this method, you can choose to plant your seeds that any time of year that you would like to.

Let's look into how you can grow seeds in your greenhouse. The most commonly used way of planting seeds in a greenhouse is through the soil. You will need a few different things for this process. You will need two containers, soil, and seeds. Each type of seed is different—but typically, all you will need to do is fill your container with soil, make a small hole for the seed, and cover it up. You will then need to water the seed often until it sprouts. Once it sprouts, you will need to continue to care for it by watering it often and making sure it has adequate light and fresh air. Growing seeds in a greenhouse is a fairly simple process, and it is basically just the same as if you were growing them inside of your house or in a garden.

You can also grow seeds in a greenhouse through hydroponics. If you choose this method, you will be planting your seeds in water or a different growing media like perlite. You will still need to make sure that your plant has what it needs before and after it sprouts.

There are a few different tools that can make growing seeds in a greenhouse much easier. The worst thing that can make growing seeds in a greenhouse easy is the type of tray that you choose to use. You can choose to use a tray that has individual pockets for each seed to grow in. These trays are nice because you know that you planted one seed in each pocket.

You can also grow your seeds in a plain, flat tray. If you choose to do this, you will just want to poke holes into the soil where you want your seeds to grow.

You will not have specific pockets for each need to go in, so you can just pick a spot. You will want to make sure that your seeds are spaced appropriately from each other so that they have space to grow.

Typically, this is the spacing that is close to 1 or 2 in part for each seed. However, the exact spacing that you need to follow will usually be listed on the back of the package of seeds. It depends on the type of seed in many circumstances.

Now that we have looked at the basics let's talk through some tips and tricks that can help you to grow the best plants from seeds. This is one way to grow seeds. There are other ways that you can do so successfully, but we believe that this method is strong and that it works well. Because of this, we are going to explain this method and details so that you are able to use it in your own greenhouse seed sowing if you want to.

You will need to get your trays ready. We recommend the trays that have a pocket for each seed. This is because they are the easiest to use. They help each plant to stay separate, and they helped to make sure that you are giving each seed enough space to grow. The trays that have separate containers for each plant have more benefits as well. For example, these trays are better at providing warmth and moisture to each separate seat. This is because the moisture and warmth stay in a certain area to protect the seed, and it does not spread out through the entire container. It is also better because it keeps the roots of each plant in its own space. If you use a tray that is flat and has many seeds in the same opening, their roots often become entwined with each other. When the roots of the plant become entwined with those of the plants around it, it hurts their survival rate greatly. This is because, in order to separate the plants, like you will have to do to move them into larger and deeper containers, you have to separate the roots. If you break the roots of the plant, it is much harder for the plant to survive. The roots are an important part of the plant, and you do not want to break them or hurt them in any way.

After you get your trays, you will want to fill them with soil. We recommend starting with a seed starting mix. This is because seed-starting mixes have all of the nutrients that you will need in order to start your seeds successfully. If you use a different type of potting mix, your seeds may still come up, but the success rate is lower than if you choose a potting mix that is specifically made for seeds and nothing else.

You can buy the seed starting mix at a store, or if you feel like making your own, you can use that option as well. If you want to make your own seed starting mix, you can start with a typical potting mix that you would find at any store. You would then want to add a few things to it. You want to add equal parts of perlite, peat moss, and organic compost. Adding these things to your regular soil will make the soil have just the right nutrients that your seedlings need to have a strong beginning of life.

Making your own soil can be a good option, especially if you are on a budget or if you simply like to make things yourself. However, it is important to know that it is best to use new soil when you are planting seedlings. If you do happen to reuse soil that you have used in seedlings or in other plans in the past, you need to sterilize this soil. This is because some germs or diseases that plants can get could be in that soil. If you plant your seedlings into the soil, they either will not sprout, or they will grow diseased plants. This is not what you want, of course. You want healthy seeds, so you will need to start with healthy soil.

Once you fill your tray with soil, it will be time to plant your seeds. You will want to push your finger into each seed pocket filled with soil to make a small indentation. Inside this hole, you will want to place two to three seeds. It made me feel silly to put 2 to 3 seeds inside each pocket when you only want one plant to grow.

However, we believe that this is the best option. This is because not every seed is going to be successful, and its mission to turn into a sea link. If you plant two to three seeds inside of each pocket, you have a much better chance that at least one of them will have enough luck in surviving. If you do happen to have two or even all three of the seeds make it and turn into seedlings, you will need to trim the seedlings that are the least strong. For example, if you have three seedlings come up in one container and one of them is tall, one of them is short, and one of them is tipping over—you will want to trim the one that is short in the one that is tipping over. This leaves the strongest and tallest seedling in your tray so that you are able to grow it into a mature plant. The strongest and tallest seedling is chosen because it has the best chance of surviving all the way through until it grows a crop and is able to be harvested from.

It is important to note that some seeds need extra care before they are planted. Larger seeds from plants like peas, pumpkins, and squash need to be soaked before they can be planted. This helps them to sprout easier and faster since they have such a hard shell. You do not want to soak all seeds, however, because small seeds like those of tomatoes and carrots can be really hard to handle after they are soaked, and they don't need to be soaked anyway. Because of this, you will want to research what each type of seed needs before you decide to plant it.

After you plant your seeds, you will want to cover them with the soil. You can either use extra soil for this or simply push the soil over that you use to make the hole earlier in the process. Either way will work just as well, so this decision is just up to your own judgment and what you feel will be easiest for you.

Once your seeds are planted and covered up with soil, it is time to care for them. In regards to the temperature of your greenhouse, most seeds germinate best if they are kept at a temperature that is between 70 and 80 degrees Fahrenheit. At night, this temperature can dip down to between 50 and 60 degrees Fahrenheit. You will want to keep your greenhouse at this temperature with either the use of sunlight or the use of heaters. If you do not have these temperatures in your greenhouse, your seeds may not do as well as you are hoping that they will do. If you have a greenhouse that is not warm enough but can still grow seedlings, you can consider something called a seedling heat mat. These are heat mats that go on the benches in your greenhouse. You can then put your trays filled with seedlings on top of them. These heat mats help the soil to stay the right temperature for the seeds. Even if the air is the wrong temperature, if the soil is the right temperature, your seedlings can have a successful start to their life.

Another trick that you can try with growing seeds is to cover your plants up before they sprout. Sometimes, seeds do best when they are covered during their germination. Once they sprout, though, you need to uncover them right away — this is because that is the time when they will start to need light to grow healthily.

Tips for growing seeds in a greenhouse is to record the results of your crops. If you grow a batch of seedlings one day after soaking your seeds in water, write down what you did to them before planting them and then write down how they end up sprouting. Compare your results to a crop that you did not soak in water.

Using this technique, you will be able to tell if you are tips and tricks that you are using for your seed starting are working or if they are not working at all.

By using this technique, you will be able to tell what works best for you and what really doesn't work. Once you have planted many batches of seeds and tried out many different tricks, you will be able to find the very best way for you to grow seedlings in your greenhouse.

Overall, growing seedlings in your greenhouse is a great thing to do. Starting plants from seeds not only saves money, but it is also a very rewarding process. You'll get to take something so small and turn it into something large. You can take one tiny seed and turn it into a plant that can feed you multiple times throughout the year. When you are growing seeds, remember to start them in either a flat open tray or a tray that has multiple openings for the seeds. Remember to put money seeds in each hole so that at least one comes out, and then pick the strongest seedling to be the one that survives. Remember to use an appropriate soil mixture for seed starting, whether that means making your own seed starting mix or buying a seed-starting potting mix from the store. Remember to keep the temperature of your greenhouse correct and make sure that your plants are getting adequate water and light. Water your plants off so that they are able to grow strong. Try out different growing techniques if you want to see if you can get your plants to grow faster than normal. Try covering your soil during the germination. Or try soaking your seeds in water before you plant them. Remember to write down your results so that you are able to compare what works and what doesn't work for you, specifically in your greenhouse. Growing seeds in your greenhouse is a great adventure, and we know that with the tips and tricks, you will be able to have great success.

Chapter 11: Useful Greenhouse Equipment

Having the right tools and equipment for this kind of job is satisfying. Having everything ready to begin your gardening adventure is somewhat essential, but you should also mentally tick off all the equipment you might need to work with your plants. Here below, I will mention some of the essential tools that you might require to operate in your garden. New technologies may help, as well. Try not to buy any piece of equipment that is not useful for your gardening; at times, it's easy to get carried away and spend more than necessary. There is an extensive list of tools below; you do not need to get them all. The trick is to get only the tools that fit the purpose of your gardening. You can always buy more tools in the future.

So, to start with some digging, we will need:

11.1 Digging Utensils

Shovel/Spade

Its always good to have a shovel or a spade, versatile tools that allow you to work them easily. If you go to the local store, you may find a wide choice of shovels, each with their own design and purpose. Generally speaking, you will use two main types of tools for punching; shovel and spade.

Sometimes people are interchanging names to these tools; however, there is a big difference between a shovel and a spade and is about their shape.

If the tool has a round edge, then you are looking at a shovel. With the rounded tip, you can dig into soil easily. I would suggest that you get a shovel that has a dish able to hold enough dirt.

If you notice that your tool has square edges, then you are looking at a spade. You can use this tool for lifting and throwing aside materials with relative ease. You can also use a spade to pat down the soil after distributing manure. This evens out the soil layer for you.

The type of tool you might require depends on how you plan to work in your garden.

A spade. With a shovel, you might get a rounded edge.

Trowel

This tool is a small excavator. This small excavator is generally used in construction areas to spread cement on surfaces. It has a similarity of use in gardening. It can be used to compact soil and transform it into layers. It also makes it possible to extract materials that you cannot otherwise with a shovel.

That does not mean that a shovel does not have enough strength to lift or break materials. It just means that sometimes, a shovel or a spade has a far reach. With that reach, you might not be able to make small adjustments to your garden wherever required.

Forks

It is a garden fork. Perhaps not so often used in gardening, it is certainly a must-have tool among your greenhouse equipment. The garden fork allows you to accomplish what you can not do with a shovel and a spade. The tool uses its handle's pullback mechanism to easily lift the soil. This is useful when you are trying to remove crops.

11.2 Cultivating tools

Cultivating it is actually the act of fertilizing the soil and taking out any unwanted plants or bad weeds.

Hoes

There is a variety of hoes out there. The options are many, but you just have to remember one essential criterion for having the right hoes: you need to get a hoe that is lightweight. Some products are really lighter than others, but you should go for one that is solid and strong. You do not want to get one that might break easily.

You also want to get a sharp one. When you use the tool, it needs to cut into the soil easily.

Weeder

A tool used to remove difficult weeds around your garden or your greenhouse.

What you should be looking for is a weeder that can work with the plants you are growing. If you are unable to decide, always ask for assistance with an expert or the supplier.

11.3 Cutting Tools

It is not always about just getting the sharpest tool in the shed. What you are looking for are tools that help you get specific tasks done. Here are some of the tools that you might require for your garden.

Pruners

You might notice that most gardeners always have pruners with them whenever they step out into a garden. What makes this tool so important?

For one, you can perform numerous tasks, including snipping off the stems of plants that you have already harvested, cutting flowers after growing them, trimming plants and shrubs, and more.

When selecting a pruner, you need to look for one that has a comfortable handle. At the same time, you should also make sure that it is lightweight. This is because heavy pruners tend to add pressure to your hands, eventually causing discomfort in the long run.

Additionally, look for pruners that have carbon steel blades. This is for the sake of durability. Other forms of material chip away easily, and you might find yourself bringing in a whetstone to sharpen the blade.

Check out the safety mechanisms of the pruner. A poor quality one might have weak springs. With weak springs, you might find yourself struggling as the spring cannot hold the pivot together. This causes the pruner to provide resistance, which makes using the tool rather uncomfortable.

Hedge Shears

Another marvelous tool for you to have, essentially, you are looking at a giant scissor-like object. They are used for cutting items and materials that you might not be able to otherwise cut using a pruner (since they are quite small, after all).

When you are looking for a hedge shear, make sure that you are looking for one that has a cushioned grip. If you have seen a shear in action, then you know that people use both hands, one on each handle provided, to work with the tool. You need something that is comfortable enough to not add unnecessary pressure on your palms.

The blade itself has to be long and sharp. There is no point in getting short-bladed hedge shears. You might as well save the money and make use of the pruner.

Lopper

Visually, a lopper is like the older, and taller, brother of the pruner. While the blades of both the pruner and the lopper have more or less the same dimensions, the handle is where the difference can be noticed. In a lopper, the handle is longer. This allows you to get into hard-to-reach places.

When looking for a lopper, make sure you get a sturdy handle, preferably made out of hardwood or steel. You should also look for rubber handles that allow you a firm and comfortable grip.

Pruning Saw

Finally, when you need to get rid of stubborn stems or weeds that need more than just clippings from pruners, shears, or loppers, then you have the pruning saw.

A lot of people actually end up borrowing a pruning saw from someone else. I do not recommend it. Firstly, the tool itself is not expensive, so you are better off getting a new one. Secondly, you need a pruning saw that is ideal for your garden, so do not look for replacements. Finally, the quality that you get from tools that are borrowed is questionable at best.

Chapter 12: How to Grow Without Soil

Growers, especially new growers, tend to wonder how true the possibility of growing plants effectively without soil is. Well, it is not only true that it is possible, but it is also more popularly practiced than one would usually assume. Growing without soil, which is also called Hydroponics, is a technique of cultivating plants using a prepared nutrient solution. The idea is that all plants generally need only light, air, water, and nutrient to grow healthily. And while the plants grown on soil would struggle to get all these necessities from the soil and the environment, they can be easily provided to them by the grower, especially in an enclosed environment such as a greenhouse. The plants can grow anywhere as long as they are supplied with the necessities for their healthy growth. Hydroponics (growing without soil) is a creative technique that offers people with non-arable lands, although interested in gardening, the chance to finally have their own garden without having to worry about the poor soil condition in their area because they won't even need to use soil at all. If you are new to this, you might want to ask how this system works, it is quite simple, and we will get right to it now:

12.1 How Does Hydroponics Work?

In this system of gardening, the roots of the plants are dipped inside a nutrient solution contained in a reservoir. The nutrient solution is pre-mixed with all the needed nutrients by the particular plant being cultivated. Using this system makes it easy to plant more in a seemingly limited space in a greenhouse. It also improves the yield at the end of the day, producing healthier products free from any diseases and pests.

There are generally 6 major methods of hydroponic system, these are Aeroponics, Wick Irrigation system, Flood and Drain, Water culture, Nutrient film technique, and Drip system.

1. Drip system: this is a method of hydroponics which employs the use of drip lines to transfer the nutrient solution directly to the base of the plants regularly. While soil is not used, a growing medium is essential in this method of hydroponics to support the plants. This method is usually used in a large-scale production garden, but for it to work effectively, it requires that each plant has its own container and invariably its own drip line. A pump system can be used (with an attached timer for automation) to take water into the drip manifold when needed. The timer is important to avoid flooding the plants and causing more harm than good in the process. A drip system can also be either a recovery system where the excess nutrient solution is recycled or a non-recovery system where the excess nutrient solution is drained off as waste instead.

2. Nutrient film technique: this method of hydroponics is usually used to grow small and quickly growing plants. The growing tray is set at an angle that enables a constant flow of the nutrient solution. The interesting thing about this method of hydroponics is that it doesn't even require a growing medium as the roots of the plants are suspended in the air. The NFT method requires the use of a pump which pumps the nutrient solution into the growing tray and also another pump connected to an air stone to ensure aeration in the nutrient solution.

3. Water Culture: this method of hydroponics is considered suitable for commercial growers interested in large-scale production because it is cheap.

It is a very simple method, if not the simplest of all methods, as the plants are placed in hanging baskets while their roots are suspended in the nutrient solution. The fact that the roots of the plants are always in the nutrient solution makes an air pump an important tool to supply oxygen for aeration in the reservoir holding the nutrient solution.

4. Flood and drain: this method is also called ebb and flow. In this method, the root system of the plants is flooded with nutrient solution intermittently, and the supply is usually controlled by a timer. When the timer is off, and the pump stops, the nutrient solution flows back down into the reservoir through the overflow tube set as a draining system. A bigger tube should be used as the overflow tube, and the grower should also keep in mind that a growing medium is needed to support the roots of the plants in this method of hydroponics.

5. Wick irrigation system: the hydroponic wick system is the easiest system to set up because there is no need for electricity or the use of a pump in the system. It's a good choice for growers just starting out with hydroponics, although it's not a suitable system for larger plants. The container which holds the plants in this method is placed on the reservoir containing the nutrient solution, and a wick is used to suck up the nutrient solution into the growing medium in the container holding the plants.

6. Aeroponics: this is said to be the most advanced method of hydroponics; it does not require a growing medium as the roots of the plants are merely suspended in the air. The suspended roots are fed by a sprinkling system set up in the nutrient solution, and the attached nozzles should be specially designed to deliver the nutrient solution in the mist form.

It is said that aeroponics gives more yield than other methods of hydroponics; this is because aeroponics allows the grower to grow more in a limited space and also because the exposed root system of the plants gives them access to more oxygen and thereby aerates faster and better. It is important to note that the roots of the plants in aeroponics tend to dry out faster and, therefore, must be fed with a nutrient solution as often as needed. A timer can be set accordingly to ease up the stress while the grower ensures that there is no power outage or provides a backup power supply in case there is a power failure.

Growing without using soil is best carried out in a greenhouse, and while it requires a bit of 'technical know-how,' the quality of the result that will be obtained cannot be overemphasized when things are done right. The right method of hydroponics should be chosen based on the purpose of gardening, and the right nutrient solution should be used for the right plant, not forgetting the use the right growing medium when the method is chosen requires one. All these are important so as to achieve successful soilless cultivation in a greenhouse.

Chapter 13: Greenhouse Environmental Control Systems

Technology advancement has made owning and running greenhouses simpler than ever before. Options of environmental control help the professional horticulturist or home gardener by automatically adjusting light intensity, humidity, and temperature from a remote location or within the greenhouse. A system of environmental control would enhance plant life within the structure by offering a continually monitored atmosphere, producing a more consistent yield.

You can automate your greenhouse environmental control systems according to your requirements. Greenhouse accessories are pre-set in phases in line with the plant's needs and gardener's choice. These systems present the most significant advantage by providing the facility to control light intensity, adjust humidity, adjust the temperature, and monitor the atmosphere, to mention some of the operations.

13.1 Accessories Controlled

Cooling systems, heating systems, fogging, systems, misting systems, vents, and fans are all controlled by control systems. The operations could be very straightforward and offer an immense benefit to keeping your greenhouses in ideal shape.

The first phase of execution could be as simple as an on/off switch to control fan circulation.

By semi-automating a control system using a timing device, a thermostat, or a humidistat, the accessories will run only when necessary; this saves energy and reduces the operating costs.

A fully automated system can be controlled through a cell phone, by remote programming system on a PC, or semaphore, saving a considerable amount of time. The fully automated system could be programmed to keep a particular set of conditions for stable plant comfort, putting into consideration the circumstances outside the structure, which might affect the growth of plants.

13.2 Advantages of Automated System

Improve Vegetation Quality: Mimicking a more cold night temperature, boosts the quality of vegetation as it more directly simulates the natural environment. Precise humidity and temperature control offer consistent growing conditions to improve production and quality.

Reduce costs of fuel: Lowering the temperature of a greenhouse at night when eighty percent of the heating takes place, lessens the consumption of energy. Centralizing temperature sensors, controlling them with a single unit prevents cooling and heating systems from running concurrently.

Increase Production: An automated system permits you to focus on growing the plants, not adjusting settings.

13.3 Advanced Accessories

Additionally to regular greenhouses accessories, environmental control systems could be programmed to contain advanced elements like remote programming, semaphore, soil sensors, photo and light sensors, drip systems, foggers, and coolers.

Your time can now be spent tending to plants instead of messing with their growing environment.

Asides the time and cost-effectiveness of the greenhouse control system, Mother Nature will also benefit. Control systems lessen the use of chemicals to aid the growth of plants as the environment is more closely adjusted to produce the perfect condition and reduce energy costs and waste. Here are some of the greenhouses advance accessories:

1. Greenhouse Benches: These benches will make performing gardening functions stress-free. Whether you're transplanting, pruning, potting, or washing farm produce, benches provide alternatives in space and height utilization. The greenhouse benches are built to complement any existing or new structure. The polyethylene grid-top and galvanized mesh offer both good drainage and air circulation while giving room for light to pass through to the plants underneath.

2. Raised Seedling Beds: Seeding beds are another fantastic accessory for greenhouses. Unlike conventional greenhouse benches, they extend growing beyond only pots. A seedling bed is about six inches deep and is supported on four legs. It is often filled with soil for growing plants. Seedling beds are the ideal way to bring a vegetable garden or flower bed straight into the greenhouse. With this, you don't have to get on your knees to plant and tend the garden as the bed is raised.

3. **Gravel Bench**: This is specially used to produce moisture. This type of bench is tailored for use in greenhouses or with plants such as orchids. You can use a fixed bench built with a metal tip rather than a conventional mesh top. To apply, fill the top of the bench with gravel and water to create a source of moisture for the flowers.

4. Grow Lights: A greenhouse such as a lean-to with low light and conventional side walls or ceiling wouldn't generate the amount of natural heat needed by specific plants. The addition of grow light is a simple solution.

There are also conversion lighting kits. The grow light permits high-pressure sodium light bulb and metal halide to be interchanged. You can rotate the bulbs as the greenhouse advances, and plant selections change. These lightings promote new growth and keep plants healthy. There are several forms of grow light in the market nowadays; for example, compact fluorescent grows light and incandescent light. Most of these models may not last long and are dangerous if water comes in contact with their bulbs. I recommend lights featuring high-pressure sodium or metal halide bulbs:

I. High-Pressure Sodium

A high-pressure sodium (HPS) bulb has a yellow glow that isn't as visually pleasing as the blue light metal halide produce. The bulbs can last for twenty-four thousand hours (about five years). HPS bulbs are suggested for greenhouses with enough lighting but want to produce more flowering plants, fruits, or vegetables.

II. Metal Halide

Metal halide bulbs emit a blue tint that mimics real sunlight and can last for twenty thousand hours. Plants become fuller when placed under a metal halide bulb. If you want to elongate daytime growing hours, the ideal option is the metal halide system as you can turn the light on before sunset and again a few hours after sunset.

5. Heat Mats: When propagating plants or starting seeds, a heat mat will be a useful propagation tool. Plug the waterproof rubber mat into an outlet to generate heat. The heat will produce warm seedling trays that will help to grow plants faster.

6. Plant Hangers: For you to take advantage of all the available space within your greenhouse, plant hangers will help just in achieving that. You can hang orchid boxes along with hanging flower baskets. You can also hang tomatoes pot if you wish. You can as well install multiple rods in your greenhouse to offer ample space, and hang many baskets from it for an ever-growing plant assortment.

13.4 Advanced Ventilation

Eave vents and ridge vents are a crucial part of any functioning greenhouse with a serviceable passive system of ventilation. When the air is not vented, it turns out to be stale, stagnant, and gives room for diseases to breed. To avoid this scenario, you need to install eave vents and ridge vents in your greenhouse. Both systems work similarly but on different parts of the greenhouse. The two units are operable panels of glass-enclosed within a frame separate from the structural framework of the greenhouse. The vent will open by a motor that is dampness-resistance or manually with the help of a rod operator. It will open to a specific direction and give room for air into the building. Both systems have screens that prevent debris and insects from gaining entrance to the greenhouse.

1. Ridge Vent: The ridge vent is essential for a greenhouse. Warm air upsurges and builds up at the top of the greenhouse. When you open the ridge vents, the warm air breaks out, and fresh, cold air breaks in. The ridge vents will also enable air circulation. If there is light wind outside, it will get into the structure and help in circulating the air; this will lessen the spread of diseases. If your greenhouse is in use of exhaust fan/intake louvers, the ridge vents will help in getting rid of hot air, so fresh air can go into the building.

2. Eave Vents: The eave vents are situated on the walls of the structure and would also open. And this allows fresh, cold air into the building. The air would spread through the room and reduce the temperature. It makes the house calmer and helps lessen the emergence of disease in greenhouse plants. You can also add rain sensors to the units so the when rain or snow hits the vents, they close automatically. If you operate an environmental control system in your greenhouse, you can program the ridge vents into your specified system. Without aeration, your greenhouse would become a glass box filled with stagnant air.

13.5 Advance Watering Systems

The perfect methods of providing your plants with essential sustenance are watering systems. Watering with the hand can become time-consuming and tedious as your plant collection grows. An automated system of watering is well-suited for plants that require high humid environments. There are several available watering systems. For example, a misting system that sprays a mist and makes the air to be saturated. The water drips are larger than the ones provided by a fogging system.

You can fit all the systems with different nozzle heads and utilize them within the same greenhouse. There are various flow rates for different nozzles so that you can create poles-apart zones. You can use a larger flowing nozzle to make sure seedlings don't dry out, while a small amount of water might be perfect for mature plants. You can program all the systems to work on a timer to control the amount of water that reaches the plants

1. Drip Misting System: You can use a drip misting system for the slow release of water. This system is perfect if you travel frequently or you have busy schedules. This system is run in such a way that it provides constant water supply to individual plants. You can fill the tubes and rearrange the holes.

2. Riser Misting System: This system is programmed for the utmost flexibility, and it's mobile. Therefore if you regularly change the layout of your greenhouse, a riser misting system will be your best option. You can place this system anywhere on the bench and move to a different area whenever you like.

3. **Suspended Misting System**: These misting systems are lifted above the benches of the greenhouse to give room for unhindered bench space. In a suspended misting system, you will directly insert the nozzles into the water source. The building runs the benches length, and it's suspended from a jack chain that you can position at any height you prefer.

4. **Retractable Hose Reels:** Water is unavoidable in any greenhouse. If you don't use a system or watering can, then the next probable option is a hose. Most gardeners are aware that hose can be bulky and occupy valuable space. When it uses a hose holder, and the unit usually twists and folds under the hose weight. To prevent these, a retractable hose reel that is mounted to a wall or rafter will help. A simple tow of the entire length of the hose retracts unit will provide a neat appearance and prevent tripping hazards. The reel turns left and right, providing maneuverability all through the greenhouse. You can also mount these units outside a greenhouse by attaching them to a garage or home.

13.6 Greenhouse Shelving

Shelving options offer additional growing and storage space for any greenhouse type. You can attach a shelf to the rafters in front of glass windows or add it to a solid wall. If there is enough space, you stack shelving on a wall. You can use this shelving for any conventional or glazed building, as they are designed to go with the aesthetics of the environment. You can turn a bay window into a miniature greenhouse by adding shelving. Garden windows usually contain several shelves for growing plants.

Best materials for shelving:

Glass: Glass is conventionally used in garden windows since it gives room for the sun to get to the shelves, and provided that you use saucers under the plants, it requires a minimal level of glass cleaning. The glass shelves would be the perfect artistic match to the façade of the window.

Wood: Wood is another aesthetically attractive option for shelving. I recommend cedar or mahogany since they can endure humidity and moisture. Once you have stained the wood, it will look like a conventional English greenhouse. Using wooden shelves will reduce sun to lower shelves, which is best for shade-loving plants like orchids.

Metal: Metal is solid and allows for the flow of air into the plant's bottom. The aluminum mesh is an excellent option for bonsai that usually demands the movement of air to thrive. Metal won't warp or rust and is a handy option for any greenhouse.

Polyethylene: Polyethylene is almost the same with metal shelving in form and benefits. The main variation is that the former is plastic with reprocessed substance. The polyethylene is black and covers dirt quickly, while metal shelving is silver.

Bench Shelving

The lower bench shelves for greenhouses are handy for plants that flourish in the shade or minimal sun conditions. These benches can be about eighteen inches deep and position beneath the existing greenhouse benches. The addition of the lower shelf increases the available growing space and provides added storage space for equipment and supplies.

Shelf Supports

The shelving supports could be either a decorative corner or a simple metal bar. Decorative corners are an ideal option when aesthetics matters. You can attach a metal bar from the above or beneath the shelf to create a hanging shelf. They are available in different forms that mimic the traditional structural design and English greenhouse.

Chapter 14: 15 Tips to Make Your Greenhouse More Efficient

The purpose and intention of the structure should be to optimize crop growth in the most efficient way possible if you own and operate a greenhouse. While it is true that numerous owners make efforts to achieve designs best suited to their needs and materials for the design they have chosen, these areas of focus will not always lead to the least energy use growth structure. All greenhouse units, regardless of their design and materials, typically serve their unique purpose in creating an optimum growth environment for different crop types.

The true purpose and goal of a greenhouse, however, should not be overlooked, and this is to create an optimal environment for growing crops that not only reduces time but also greatly saves money.

In this guide, 15 tips are offered to help you achieve a high degree of efficiency and energy reduction for your greenhouse.

1. Build Conservation. Checklist Conservation is an essential component of basic operation at the cost of high energy use of today's greenhouses. Research suggests that the energy consumed by greenhouses is: 75% of total energy in relation to heating and/or cooling, 15% of the total energy in connection with the supply of electricity to the unit, 10% of the total energy in respect of resources needed for service and servicing.

Based on these figures, it is only sensible to begin with a conservation checklist that emphasizes energy consumers who could save the most. This means you should focus on ways to increase efficiency in climate control and electricity use. The first step towards making your greenhouse more efficient is knowing what to focus on and where to start.

2. Assess the structure. The second step in the development of an efficient greenhouse is the assessment of the structure as a whole. This is particularly important if you concentrate on climate control. Cool air or warm air can easily escape from the greenhouse. When trying to keep a certain temperature in the greenhouse, you should understand that your losses will depend on the structure cover and the age of the unit. If you want to heat the structure effectively, consider a double polyethylene cover–which can reduce your heating costs by 50 percent. When using a glass greenhouse, consider upgrading the structure with a double polyethylene layer–which could reduce costs up to 60%.

3. Eliminate air leaks. It is imperative that you work to prevent any air leaks associated with the structure to ensure that your greenhouse is operating efficiently. The main place to begin is the structure door or doors. A special door closing unit should be used, or even door spring mounted to make sure the air does not enter the unit. Weatherstripping should also be placed around the unit openings, like doors, windows, and ventilation units. The strip should also be placed around openings close to fans. If you find holes in the greenhouse siding or Foundation, they should be repaired immediately.

4. If you want to increase the efficiency of your greenhouse, you should focus on doubling the structure coverage.

One way to do this is to bubble-wrap the interior walls of the structure. It offers what is called a "thermopane effect" in the device that improves Insulation in the house.

If you have an older frame, just throw a double plastic sheet over the device to reduce the infiltration and minimize heat loss by up to 50 percent.

5. Implement a conserving curtain. If you want an efficient greenhouse, consider a thermal curtain. Such goods will save from 20 to 50 percent everywhere. If the cost of the curtain is around $2.50 on average for each square foot, the payback is paid in two years. If it costs less, you will be paid sooner.

6. Install Insulation at the Foundation. You should take the time to insulate your Foundation to reduce the efficiency of your greenhouse — the best way to use a board made of polyurethane or polystyrene. The board should be 1 to 2 inches thick and should be placed under the ground approximately 8 inches to help reduce heat loss. In this way, the soil located on the region close to the sides of the structure in the winter months will increase to a total of 10.

7. When you are interested in increasing the amount of heat stored in your greenhouse, the area behind your heating pipes should be isolated. Nevertheless, it is better to use aluminum-faced building paper to help radiate heat from the pipes back onto the growing area of your greenhouse.

8. Consider the location of your structure

To reduce your greenhouse energy consumption, but the structure in an area surrounded by trees and/or other types of structures. The wind that the unit undergoes over time is a result of a lot of heat loss with growth structures. If you choose to put the building in a sheltered area, it is important to make sure the building always receives the correct light so that the crops continue to grow properly.

9. The next step in optimizing greenhouse energy efficiency is to place windbreaks on the north side of the edifice as well as on the northwest side. In these areas, you might put several coniferous trees or even a plastic snow fence. This reduces the amount of heat loss by wind exposure.

10. Increase the amount of space in your Greenhouse One of the most productive ways to maximize greenhouse efficiency is to increase your unit space. You can improve the amount of space you have up to 90 percent with benches that can be moved or peninsular shaped. You should mount racks that can be stacked if you have small plants. Furthermore, in baskets that can be placed on rails or on overhead transport systems, you can grow crops.

11. Regular heating system maintenance if you want to save time and money by optimizing the greenhouse efficiency, make sure your heating system maintains regularly. You should make sure the boiler works optimally and is periodically cleaned. You should have a furnace regularly changed and washed. If you have a medium unit, this may save hundreds of gallons of petroleum per year.

12. Use Electronic Thermostats you should convert to an electronic model if you currently use an electronic thermostat. In so doing, you will find that up to five hundred gallons of heating fuel can be saved each year. The implementation of these thermostats will also lead to more precise temperature measurements. Mechanical units have been measured to read sometimes up to two degrees higher than electronic devices. This could result in expenses exceeding $200.00 per year. You can avoid paying too much to control your structure's climate by switching to an electronic thermostat.

13. Install fans the next way to maximize the output of the greenhouse is to install fans generating horizontal airflow.

14. Try using open-roof cooling strategies. When you spend a lot of money cooling your greenhouse, you can try open-roof designs. This form of design removes the need for fans and high-priced refrigeration systems.

15. Finally, if you want to optimize your greenhouse efficiency, you should install energy lighting systems. The use of moving bulbs and lights is known to be efficient devices that save you hundreds of dollars per year.

Chapter 15: Maintaining Your Greenhouse

The effort applied in keeping a thing in its proper condition is referred to as maintenance. It refers to actions carried out in order to prevent a hazard from happening and can also refer to actions taken in order to reverse a negative effect and restore back to the proper condition. Before starting your greenhouse garden, it is important to know how to maintain it. It is even arguable that more than knowing how to start your greenhouse garden, it is much more important to know how to maintain it. This is because the success of the plants you are growing depends on your ability to maintain the greenhouse. This will provide you with useful tips on how to maintain your greenhouse garden so you can be fully ready to get started with your own greenhouse. Remember that the purpose of creating a greenhouse is to provide a conducive growing environment for your plants and protect them against adverse weather conditions. It is then expected that plants grown in a greenhouse should outperform the ones grown in an open field. The greenhouse gives you the opportunity to successfully cultivate plants that are normally not suitable for your environment. The many benefits a greenhouse garden offers should be enough motivation to works towards maintaining it so as to get the best of it. Maintaining your greenhouse may and may not be expensive; the cost of greenhouse maintenance depends on many factors. The size of your greenhouse and the type of plants being grown are major determinants, and therefore it is wise to choose a greenhouse whose maintenance is within the available capital. For new growers, maintaining the greenhouse may seem difficult, but with time and the right understanding, it becomes a very easy thing to do.

15.1 How to maintain the right Temperature in the Greenhouse

Regardless of the size of your greenhouse, the system temperature is one of the important factors that determine successful cultivation. Below are tips on how to maintain the right greenhouse temperature:

1. Install sensors or, better yet, monitoring system in your greenhouse. This will help to monitor the change in the temperature of your greenhouse. Some sensors will also give feedback on the moisture level of your greenhouse.

2. Ensure sufficient ventilation. The enclosed greenhouse can sometimes create a heated growing environment; sufficient ventilation is then needed to keep the right temperature range. Install cooling systems such as fans or air conditioners depending on your greenhouse size and plant type.

3. Pay attention to your lighting in the system. Depending on the external weather condition, adjust your greenhouse lighting accordingly to maintain the right temperature. You may Install grow lights if necessary, and you may also want to consider installing heaters.

15.2 How to maintain the right relative Humidity in a Greenhouse

The humidity here refers to the amount of moisture in the greenhouse growing environment. It is no news that keeping the wrong humidity in the greenhouse is detrimental to the growth of the plants. Here are a few tips on how to maintain the right relative humidity:

1. Avoid overwatering your growing medium. Too much watering is the beginning of trouble in the plants' root

system. The humidity level in the greenhouse increases when there is too much water in the medium.

2. Ensure enough air circulation. This will improve the ventilation in the greenhouse and invariably ensure the right humidity level.

15.3 Maintaining your Greenhouse in Cold weather

Keeping the greenhouse in the right condition can be a bit extreme in cold weather, especially during the winter season. However, the following tips can help to easily maintain your greenhouse during this period:

1. Use a thermostat to monitor your greenhouse temperature level in order to know how much heat you need to supply.

2. Install a heater in your greenhouse. This is very helpful in an extremely cold climate. Heat up your greenhouse environment to the needed degree to keep your plants healthy but keep in mind that even in the cold season, the weather condition changes during day time and night time and therefore installs a good and reliable thermometer, which will indicate the temperature changes accurately.

3. Another tip is to ensure that your heater size is sufficient to cover your entire plantation. If your greenhouse is too large for the heater size, you may demarcate your greenhouse and heat up the area suitable for the heater size for effectiveness.

With the right temperature, light intensity, and humidity put in place in the greenhouse system, other required maintenance comes down to frequent inspection to ensure a tidy environment, pest-free plants, and if there is any error, quickly making adjustments before it becomes a bigger issue. Keep in mind that when it comes to greenhouse gardening, consistency is the key. If all these maintenance guidelines seem a bit too much for you at first, keep at it because it only gets better and easier in greenhouse gardening.

Conclusion

A greenhouse is a must-have for any gardener. It has so many potential uses and makes your life so much easier than you will wonder how you ever managed without one.

You can spend as much money as you want on your greenhouse; it depends on your budget. However, what is important is that you choose the site and then prepare it properly. Doing so will reduce the amount of maintenance you need to do and extend the lifespan of your greenhouse.

Your greenhouse needs to be secure against the wind and any potential damage from the surroundings, think footballs, and falling branches. Take care of setting it up properly, then it will be very low maintenance and an absolute pleasure to grow in.

Your seed may be planted earlier in the year and grow delicate crops longer into the cooler months. For anyone outside of the warmest areas, it is essential as it will make the difference when it comes to getting your crops to produce a viable harvest.

You will now be able to set up your greenhouse and manage it easily. It will reduce the amount of work you need to do and allow you to grow plants that would otherwise have been out of your reach.

You do have to remember that greenhouses come with their own potential set of problems. However, most of these can be avoided purely by ensuring there are suitable ventilation and air circulation. These two issues are by far the number one cause of problems within any glasshouse.

It is vital that you either have a suitable irrigation system in your greenhouse or that you water your plants regularly. On hotter days, they will require daily watering, particularly if they are in smaller containers. Lack of water causes leaf, flower, and fruit drop, which will impact your potential harvest.

If you are planning on putting a greenhouse in your garden or on your allotment, then I'd recommend you go and size it up. Look for a suitable space and measure it up to determine what size greenhouse you can put in. You may decide to start with a portable greenhouse or a hoop house, depending on the space and budget available to you.

Making the decisions about the type of floor and foundation need to be made right at the start as these are very difficult and expensive to change later on. I wouldn't recommend growing directly in the soil as it will quickly become a burden and turn your greenhouse into a chore.

I will guarantee that in your first year, you will overcrowd your greenhouse in your excitement. By the second, you will want another greenhouse or a bigger one as you understand the benefits and how great a greenhouse is. I'm currently looking at putting a second greenhouse on my plot and a 25-foot long polytunnel (hoop house). I can see so many benefits, and after a couple of poor growing years, this will make a massive difference to my ability to produce the more delicate crops I like.

Owning a greenhouse is a lot of fun and full of potential. I would highly recommend you get one, as large as you can afford and fit in. You will enjoy it immensely as it allows you to be successful grow a wide variety of crops that you would otherwise have struggled to grow. These useful glasshouses are well worth the investment and will give you years of enjoyment and growing pleasure.

Lightning Source UK Ltd.
Milton Keynes UK
UKHW020653131020
371498UK00013B/542